ned
ds,
vel.

our
ets
rld,
of
experience and a passion for travel.

**Rely on Thomas Cook as your
travelling companion on your next trip
and benefit from our unique heritage.**

Thomas Cook **pocket** guides

TORONTO
Laura Trethewey

Your travelling companion since 1873

Thomas
Cook

Written by Laura Trethewey

Published by Thomas Cook Publishing
A division of Thomas Cook Tour Operations Limited
Company registration No: 3772199 England
The Thomas Cook Business Park, 9 Coningsby Road
Peterborough PE3 8SB, United Kingdom
Email: books@thomascook.com, Tel: +44 (0)1733 416477
www.thomascookpublishing.com

Produced by The Content Works Ltd
Aston Court, Kingsmead Business Park, Frederick Place
High Wycombe, Bucks HP11 1LA
www.thecontentworks.com

Series design based on an original concept by Studio 183 Limited

ISBN: 978-1-84848-295-1

First edition © 2010 Thomas Cook Publishing
Text © Thomas Cook Publishing
Maps © Thomas Cook Publishing/PCGraphics (UK) Limited
Transport map © Communicarta Limited

Series Editor: Kelly Anne Pipes
Production/DTP: Steven Collins

Printed and bound in Spain by GraphyCems

Cover photography (CN Tower) © SCPhotos/Alamy

All rights reserved. No part of this publication may be reproduced, stored in a retrieval
system or transmitted, in any form or any means, electronic, mechanical, recording
or otherwise, in any part of the world, without prior permission of the publisher.
Requests for permission should be made to the publisher at the above address.

Although every care has been taken in compiling this publication, and the contents
are believed to be correct at the time of printing, Thomas Cook Tour Operations
Limited cannot accept any responsibility for errors or omission, however caused,
or for changes in details given in the guidebook, or for the consequences of any
reliance on the information provided. Descriptions and assessments are based on
the author's views and experiences when writing and do not necessarily represent
those of Thomas Cook Tour Operations Limited.

CONTENTS

INTRODUCING TORONTO

Introduction..................................6
When to go...................................8
Queen Street West....................12
History...14
Lifestyle......................................16
Culture..18

MAKING THE MOST OF TORONTO

Shopping.....................................22
Eating & drinking......................24
Entertainment & nightlife 28
Sport & relaxation 30
Accommodation 34
The best of Toronto 40
Suggested itineraries................42
Something for nothing..............44
When it rains 46
On arrival...................................48

THE CITY OF TORONTO

Downtown 58
West Side 76
East Side.....................................92

OUT OF TOWN TRIPS

The Niagara region....................106
Stratford 118

PRACTICAL INFORMATION

Directory......................................128
Emergencies................................138

INDEX...140

MAPS

Toronto 50
Toronto transport map................54
Downtown 60
West End 78
East End 94
Around Toronto 108

SYMBOLS KEY

The following symbols are used throughout this book:

ⓐ address ⓣ telephone ⓦ website address ⓛ opening times
ⓝ public transport connections ⓘ important

The following symbols are used on the maps:

𝒊	information office	■	points of interest
✈	airport	O	city
✚	hospital	O	large town
🛡	police station	○	small town
🚍	bus station	══	motorway
🚆	railway station	—	main road
Ⓜ	subway	—	minor road
✝	cathedral	—	railway
❶	numbers denote featured cafés & restaurants		

Hotels and restaurants are graded by approximate price as follows:
£ budget price ££ mid-range price £££ expensive

Abbreviations used in this guide:

St	Street	E	East
Rd	Road	W	West
Ave	Avenue	S	South
Blvd	Boulevard		

ⓞ *Toronto skyline at sunset*

INTRODUCING
Toronto

Introduction

Rather than basking in nationalist pride, Canada's most populous city revels in its multiculturalism and diversity. Around half of the population was born outside Canada and more than 140 languages and dialects are spoken in the city alone – extraordinary statistics considering the fact that, until as recently as the 1950s, Toronto mainly comprised white, Anglo-Saxon residents and was famous for its upright Protestant character. Many of the immigrants arrived seeking refuge from war: Europeans from the ravages of World War II, Eastern Europeans from the Soviet Union, Vietnamese from South Vietnam. Economic migrants soon followed and the city's most common mother tongue after English is now Chinese, followed by Italian and Punjabi. In the past few decades, Toronto has become a land of possibility for everyone: newly-arrived immigrants, fourth-generation Torontonians and world travellers simply here for a visit.

Part of Toronto's appeal is that, clichés aside, it really does offer something for everyone. Foodies, fashion savants, culture addicts, thrill seekers and budget travellers will all feel comfortable here. The restaurant scene, in particular, is renowned for its mash-up of flavours as well as its commitment to local, organic food. 'Starchitects' – shorthand for celebrity architects – like Frank Gehry and Daniel Libeskind have put their stamp on the city's top cultural institutions, while local authors such as Michael Ondaatje and Margaret Atwood write love stories to the city.

Investment is pouring in, swanky new buildings are rising up, bike lanes and improved transit services are in the works, and dozens of heritage projects, festivals and markets are appearing all the time. A renewed focus on green spaces is transforming the city's parks into hubs of activity. Now, more than ever, is the time to visit this bustling, energetic city – truly a city on the rise.

🔺 *A Chinese festival is just one of the celebrations of multicultural Toronto*

When to go

Toronto hibernates during the winter months, as the days are short and the streets wet and slippery. Arrive at the end of April to find the city springing back into life, with cafés spilling out onto the sidewalks and impromptu street concerts taking place. Spring and autumn are the best times to enjoy Toronto with decent weather and relatively few tourists.

SEASONS & CLIMATE

Toronto's weather is moderated by Lake Ontario, making the winter more bearable than in much of Canada, but it still gets absolutely freezing cold. In January and February, the average temperature hovers around -4°C (25°F), rising to just under 10°C (50°F) in April. Snow covers the ground from December to March but is quickly cleared from streets. In July, expect temperatures of around 22°C (72°F), with the odd day rising to over 30°C (86°F). Summer lasts pretty much until the end of September, but come November, thermometers have plummeted once more to a chilly 4°C (39°F).

ANNUAL EVENTS
January–February
Come Up To My Room An alternative design show in January, in which an entire floor of the Gladstone Hotel is transmogrified by up-and-coming designers. ⓐ 1214 Queen St W ⓦ www.comeuptomyroom.com

Winterlicious For two weeks at the beginning of February, Toronto's top restaurants offer cut-rate, prix fixe meals.

March–April

Canadian Music Week Just about every notable Canadian musical act performs in the span of five days in mid-March.
📞 905-858-4747 🌐 www.cmw.net

HotDocs Usually held at the start of April, this documentary film festival is starting to rival September's TIFF in popularity.
🌐 www.hotdocs.ca

⬥ *The waterfront at night during the Luminato Festival*

May–July

Doors Open Over 100 historic buildings open their doors to the public over one weekend in late May. Ⓦ www.toronto.ca/doorsopen

Luminato Festival The Luminato Festival of Arts & Creativity in June is exactly that – ten days of mostly free, public celebrations of the creative arts in Toronto's Downtown streets, stages and parks. Ⓦ www.luminato.com

North By North East The northern cousin to the South By South West festival in Texas offers cutting-edge films and bands in mid-June. Ⓦ www.nxne.com

Gay Pride A massive jaunt down Yonge Street in late June or July, complete with occasional public nudity, street dancing and water fights. Ⓦ www.pridetoronto.com

Toronto Fringe Festival Toronto's largest theatre festival takes place over the first two weeks of July: tickets go for just $10. Ⓦ www.fringetoronto.com

Caribana A month-long Caribbean festival in July, with reggae, samba, djembe, salsa and zouk in Toronto's main streets. Ⓦ www.caribanafestival.com

August–October

Beerlicious Over 200 brewers turn up for this August drink-a-thon, where ticket-holders are let into a vast arena to sample lagers, ales, stouts and pale ales. Ⓦ www.beerfestival.ca

Nuit Blanche Massive crowds overwhelm this all-night cross-city art show in early October. Ⓦ www.scotiabanknuitblanche.ca

Toronto International Film Festival (TIFF) September's renowned film festival is not just about red carpet and A-listers. Snag a ticket to a great indie flick premiere here. Ⓦ www.tiff.net

Word on the Street On the last Sunday of September, this literary festival takes over the Queen's Park circle, with major publishers setting up tables alongside indie presses. Ⓦ www.thewordonthestreet.ca

November–December
The Royal Agricultural Winter Fair Held every November, this kitschy fair features giant vegetable competitions, horse jumping and livestock contests. Ⓦ www.royalfair.org
One of a Kind Show Nigh on 800 designers and artisans sell their unique crafts and clothes, making this an ideal place to pick up a holiday gift. Ⓦ www.oneofakindshow.com

PUBLIC HOLIDAYS
New Year's Day 1 Jan
Family Day 15 Feb 2010, 21 Feb 2011, 20 Feb 2012
Good Friday 2 Apr 2010, 22 Apr 2011, 6 Apr 2012
Easter Monday 5 Apr 2010, 25 Apr 2011, 9 Apr 2012
Victoria Day 24 May 2010, 23 May 2011, 21 May 2012
Canada Day 1 July
Civic Holiday 2 Aug 2010, 2 Aug 2011, 1 Aug 2012
Labour Day 6 Sept 2010, 6 Sept 2011, 5 Sept 2012
Thanksgiving Day 11 Oct 2010, 11 Oct 2011, 10 Oct 2012
Remembrance Day 11 Nov
Christmas Day & Boxing Day 25 & 26 Dec

Queen Street West

Queen Street West, often referred to simply as Queen West, is an ever-changing cultural mecca. Originally known as Lot Street until the 1800s, it was renamed in honour of Queen Victoria and soon became populated by Irish immigrants. By the early 1900s, a Jewish community had settled in the area as well. The street's trendy beginnings occurred in the 1950s and 1960s, when the first boutiques and bars starting popping up, and reached its high point in the 1980s with the music video channel **MuchMusic** (Ⓦ www.muchmusic.com) at Queen and John attracting hordes of musicians and creative types, while nearby **Ontario College of Art & Design** (OCAD Ⓦ www.ocad.ca) artists trickled in. All this changed a decade later when The Gap and other big chains moved in, driving rents up and forcing the little guys out. One of the last remaining vestiges of this earlier era, Pages Bookstore, which opened in 1979, closed in the summer of 2009 due to escalating rents.

The cultural cache of the street is still alive and well, however, just a little bit further west down the street. While 'Queen West' refers to the whole drag, 'West Queen West' has now been coined to mean more specifically the area after Trinity Bellwoods Park. Here, it seems that each storefront belongs to a hot new designer, art gallery or restaurant. There are signs that the creep west is continuing, as the once dangerous Parkdale neighbourhood at the edge of West Queen West fills with bistros and vintage shops. The Gladstone Hotel (see page 37) serves as a meeting point for residents, who have banded together to fight the onslaught of condos and big-box chains that usurped the previous Queen

West. For now, the area is holding strong as the central hub of Toronto's alternative art scene.

🔺 *The intriguing Ontario College of Art & Design building*

History

Before the first Europeans came to the area in 1615, the Toronto region was home to several aboriginal tribes. French and English fur traders began passing through in the 1700s, when a French trading post was established. In 1787, the land was bought from the Mississauga tribe (now the name of a western suburb) for the princely sum of 2,000 gun flints, 24 brass kettles, 120 looking glasses, 24 lace hats, a bale of flowered flannel, 96 gallons of rum and a small amount of British pounds.

On 13 July 1793, John Graves Simcoe, the freshly-appointed Lieutenant-Governor of Upper Canada, chose the site as the new naval base for the British because of its natural harbour and protected bay. In order to establish a British presence in the area, he named the city York. The town grew slowly until the 1820s and 1830s, when a flood of British immigrants increased the population fivefold. The City of Toronto was officially founded in 1834 with a population of 9,000.

In 1837, a rebellion led by William Lyon Mackenzie, the future first mayor of Toronto, sprang up. Mackenzie, a fiery Scotsman who emigrated from the States, gathered together a band of rebels to challenge the Family Compact– a group of high-ranking, influential British families that ran the city. The rebellion failed pitifully, with a few of the rebels killed in a shoot-out.

Toronto's population and wealth continued to grow throughout the 1900s, reaching 200,000 people by the turn of the 20th century. The first electric streetcar, now a trademark of Toronto streets, ran down Church Street in 1892. By World War II, Toronto's population began to grow until it outstripped that of all other

Canadian cities, and it soon became an economic powerhouse with a formidable financial sector concentrated in the Downtown Bay Street area.

For most of its existence the city was British and Protestant, but after World War II a huge influx of immigrants flowed in. Today, more than half the population is born somewhere other than Canada. Although Toronto's unbridled growth has established the city as a place of opportunity and diversity, its buildings and history have been the victim of this prosperity. Huge swathes of the city are either concrete or skyscraper, with no trace of its rich history. Fortunately, over the last few decades, an urban reform movement, sparked by American urbanist Jane Jacobs, has sprouted with a renewed interest in preserving old buildings rather than tearing them down.

⬤ *The sun sets on Toronto's old City Hall*

Lifestyle

Toronto goes by a few names: the self-deprecating 'Hogtown', the PR-friendly 'the city that works', and the more modern 'T.dot'. In its moral Victorian days, it was known as Toronto the Good. But however Toronto's residents view their city, the rest of the country sees Toronto as the business capital of Canada.

The city's trademark is ambition. Each Torontonian seems to have a million plans and goals he or she wants to accomplish that very minute. Many people juggle second jobs and hobbies around a regular, 9-to-5 working week, whether it be DJing at a club or hosting a knitting club. This means at the end of the week, most opt for relaxing pursuits like unwinding over a meal, an evening of cocktails, a concert or a movie. A younger crowd heads to Clubland, the party district between Queen and King Street, for all-night dancing.

Brunch, as the New York Times has noted, is "practically a competitive sport in Toronto" with locals packing out the city's favourite brunch spots on Saturday mornings. Sitting around in cafés, chatting with the barista and ordering multiple lattes, is another favourite weekend activity. Over the last few years, residents have been starting to make much more use of their public spaces, with farmers' markets popping up all over the city and families spending more time in public parks and gardens.

Even in the country's largest city, the maxim about Canadian friendliness holds true. It's common to see businessmen holding the door for one another on Bay Street, or a punk teenager giving up her seat to an elderly lady on the subway. Torontonians tend to be a shade shy, but after a little persuasion they'll readily open up as friendly, generous people. And in terms of culture, you couldn't find a better place to visit: whether it's film, literature, fashion, art, food or design you're after, all roads lead here.

◉ *Weekends are especially popular times for catching up over a coffee*

Culture

Despite Toronto's famed diversity, it's still possible to distinguish clearly – even geographically – between the established 'higher' arts and the more DIY indie scene. Downtown holds the high-art institutions such as the Art Gallery of Ontario (see page 66), Royal Ontario Museum (see page 68), and **Four Seasons Centre** (ⓐ 145 Queen St W ⓣ 416-363-8231 ⓦ www.coc.ca), which houses the Canadian Opera Company in the country's first ever purpose-built opera theatre. On the western and eastern fringes of the city, you'll discover the more alternative arts spaces.

The main hub for art galleries lies along Queen Street West, past Trinity Bellwoods Park and around the Queen and Ossington intersection. The theatre district runs along King Street West from Spadina Avenue over to University Avenue, with another stretch around the Yonge and Queen intersection which includes the **Elgin & Winter Garden Theatres** (ⓐ 189 Yonge St ⓣ 416-314-2901 ⓦ www.heritagefdn.on.ca) and **Canon Theatre** (ⓐ 263 Yonge St ⓣ 416-872-1212 ⓦ www.mirvish.com). Nearby is the alternative **Factory Theatre** (ⓐ 125 Bathurst St ⓣ 416-504-9971 ⓦ www.factorytheatre.ca), while Toronto's classical theatre **SoulPepper** (ⓐ 55 Mill Street, Building 49 ⓣ 416-203-6264 ⓦ www.soulpepper.ca) is in the Distillery District.

Chief among multi-purpose cultural centres is the fantastic **Harbourfront Centre** (ⓐ 235 Queens Quay W ⓣ 416-973-4000 ⓦ www.harbourfrontcentre.com), a 10-acre site on the waterfront which contains the Fleck Dance Theatre (see page 67) and Power Plant gallery (see page 68). Live music performances tend to be fairly scattered, with the smaller acts appearing at popular

⬥ The Elgin and Winter Garden Theatres on Yonge Street

ROM VS AGO

In June 2008, the Royal Ontario Museum (ROM) put the finishing touches on a massive $320 million renovation, which saw American architect Daniel Libeskind adorning the building with huge panels of glass and steel. Not to be outdone, the Art Gallery of Ontario (AGO) then revealed its own $276 million renovation by Toronto-born architect Frank Gehry. Debate rages, with many preferring the fine wood interiors of the AGO to the ROM's jarring angles. It's started a trend: the Royal Conservatory of Music (see below) recently surprised residents with a revamp by Toronto-based KPMB, which also redesigned the Gardiner Museum of Ceramic Art (see page 67).

places such as Lee's Palace (see page 74) and Sneaky Dee's (see page 89). As well as the Four Seasons Centre, it's worth checking out the **Royal Conservatory of Music** (🅰 273 Bloor St W 🅣 416-408 2824 🅦 www.rcmusic.ca), one of the oldest classical music schools in the country, which holds regular public concerts. To find out where classical concerts are taking place, check *Wholenote* magazine's useful website 🅦 www.thewholenote.com.

▶ *Inside the sparkling Winter Garden Theatre (see page 18)*

MAKING THE MOST OF
Toronto

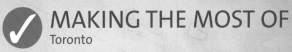

Shopping

Vintage, bespoke, designer or mass retail – Toronto has it all and at a good price. The main shopping strips run along Queen Street and Bloor Street West, with each having a completely different flavour.

If you have a bit of money in your pocket or just like to window-shop around top designers, head to Bloor Street West, between Yonge and Spadina. Here you'll find the city's pricier shops such as Holt Renfrew (see page 70), a chic retailer with all the big names plus a special selection of designers from around the world. Not far from here is Yorkville, Toronto's equivalent of New York's SoHo but with more trees. Fashionistas can easily while away an afternoon perusing the tiny boutiques. Around the corner at Hazelton Lanes, Yorkville's shopping mall, are brands like Hugo Boss, Vivienne Westwood and Yves Saint Laurent. Further along Bloor, past Spadina and into the Annex neighbourhood, are where you'll find more independent retailers, such as the

MONEY-SAVING CARDS
Save money for shopping by purchasing a **CityPass** (ⓦ www.citypass.com). For $59 ($39 children under 12), it offers free entry into most major sites for nine days. Another option is the **GO Toronto Card** (ⓘ 1-866-629-4335 ⓦ www.smartdestinations.com), which includes a handy hop-on, hop-off bus tour as well as free entry to 18 attractions in Toronto and the Niagara Falls.

● *The Eaton Centre has plenty of shopping options*

record store **Sonic Boom** (ⓐ 512 Bloor St W ⓣ 416-532-0334
ⓦ www.sonicboommusic.com ⓛ 10.00–00.00) and the famous
comic book shop **The Beguiling** (ⓐ 601 Markham St ⓣ 416-533-9168
ⓦ www.beguiling.com ⓛ 11.00–19.00 Mon–Thur, Sat, 11.00–21.00
Fri, 12.00–18.00 Sun).

Queen Street West, starting at the Eaton Centre, is a sea of
chain stores in gleaming glass-fronted buildings. Further west,
past Trinity Bellwoods Park, a slew of boutiques begin to appear
tucked in between the art galleries. For vintage stores head to
Kensington Market, where shop after shop is bursting with
funky used clothing, or walk the stretch of Ossington Avenue
between Queen Street West and Dundas West.

Eating & drinking

Multicultural as it is, Toronto's claim to foodie fame is its ability to mash up any and every culinary style. It's still possible, however, to pinpoint areas of the city where restaurants specialise in a certain type of national cuisine. Chinatown runs down Spadina Avenue between College Street and Queen Street West, with great Vietnamese, Korean and Japanese restaurants nestling among the typical Cantonese eateries. 'Little Italy' runs from Bathurst Street west along College Street, with old Italian pizzerias such as **Café Diplomatico** (ⓐ 594 College St ❶ 416-534-4637 ⓦ www.diplomatico.ca ❶ 08.00–02.00 Thur–Sat, 08.00–01.00 Sun–Wed) ruling the roost. 'Little Poland' stretches down Roncesvalles to King Street. Despite the rough divisions there are exceptions to all these areas, so it's not unusual to find a killer Jewish deli like **Caplansky's Deli** (ⓐ 356 College St ❶ 416-500-3852 ⓦ www.caplanskys.com), for example, smack bang in the middle of Little Italy.

If there's one meal of the day that Torontonians love, it's brunch. If they don't have time for the full works hash-browns-eggs-benny treatment, a gourmet farmers' market breakfast

PRICE CATEGORIES
Price ratings in this guide indicate the approximate cost of a main course and drink for one person, not including tax or tip.
£ up to $30 ££ $30–60 £££ over $60

🔺 *The Victory Café (see page 91) is a quiet little bar in Toronto's West End*

sandwich is the next best thing. **Carousel Bakery** (ⓐ 93 Front St E
ⓣ 416-863-6764) inside the St Lawrence Market serves wonderful
peameal bacon sandwiches. Incidentally, 'peameal' bacon is a
Canadian speciality you must try: a piece of unsmoked back
bacon rolled in a coating of ground peas or cornmeal.

Another favourite foodie trend involves sharing platters and
tapas-style dining, a great way for groups of friends to nibble over
drinks until the early hours. Be cautious if you're on a budget,
though, as this can sometimes be more expensive than a single
entrée. In recent years, Montreal's culinary style has gained a
strong foothold in Toronto with its penchant for charcuterie,
poutine (french fries, curd cheese and gravy) and unpasteurised
cheese. Check out **Taste of Quebec** (ⓐ 55 Mill St, Building 32
ⓣ 416-364-5020 ⓦ www.atasteofquebec.com) in the Distillery

🔺 *Enjoy a beer at the historic Mill Street Brewery (see page 64)*

STREET FOOD

For far too long the city streets only offered hot dogs – although, to be fair, they were darn good hot dogs, ranging from honking fat Polish sausages to spicy Italian and vegan dogs served with olives and sauerkraut. Ethnic food is now starting to break into the street food market, however, with anything from Persian biryani and Greek *souvlaki* (skewered kebabs) to Korean *bulgogi* (marinated barbecued beef), spicy chapli kebabs and Caribbean jerk chicken.

District, where you can sample tons of Francophone favourites and stock up on maple syrup, apple cider and soft cheeses.

Restaurants are discovering that locals like to drink local wine, so look for the VQA label that guarantees its Ontario or British Columbia origin. Stand-out wines to try while you're here include those from Inniskillin, Peller Estates and Jackson-Triggs, all based near Niagara-on-the-Lake (see page 113). Although Canadian ice wines (a sweet wine produced from grapes which are frozen while still on the vine) are pricey, they really are the nectar of the gods, so pick a day to celebrate and splurge on a bottle.

Make sure to reserve a table at popular restaurants ahead of time, as it's common for some places to be booked out for weeks, if not months, on end. A tip of around 15 per cent is expected in most restaurants; in cafés and bars you can get away with less. Smoking is banned in all public places and enclosed workplaces, including bars, restaurants and clubs, as well as on patios where there's an awning or overhang. Check signs before lighting up.

Entertainment & nightlife

However you like to spend your evenings, Toronto can do it: from calm and relaxing to an all-night marathon of dancing, drinking and music. The club district runs along Richmond West, starting at John Street. Around Bay Street are jazz holes and resto-lounges that specialise in sharing platters for the moneyed, after-work crowd. Ossington Avenue has blossomed into the latest hotspot for bar-hopping and cocktail-swilling. The College Street area around Bathurst, also known as Little Italy, also transforms at night into a stretch of bars and clubs. Note that the age limit for visiting clubs and bars is 19; take ID even if you're in your 20s.

Each neighbourhood has its own cinema, with the **Revue Cinema** (ⓐ 400 Roncesvalles Ave ❶ 416-531-9950 Ⓦ www.revuecinema.ca) in the West End, the vintage **Fox Theatre** (ⓐ 2236 Queen St E ❶ 416-691-7330 Ⓦ http://foxtheatre.ca) in the East End, and the **Bloor Cinema** (ⓐ 506 Bloor St W

WHAT'S ON?

Stillepost (Ⓦ www.stillepost.com) is the best listings website for alternative as well as mainstream music in Toronto, while *BlogTO* (Ⓦ www.blogto.com) and *Martini Boys* (Ⓦ www.martiniboys.com) have comprehensive listings that cover art, music and dance. The central ticketing hubs are **TOtix** (Ⓦ www.totix.com), which offers discounted last-minute tickets to events, and **Ticketmaster** (❶ 416-872-5000 Ⓦ www.ticketmaster.ca).

🔺 *Toronto has an energetic club scene*

🕿 416-516-2331 Ⓦ www.bloorcinema.com) in the Annex 'hood.
Every Saturday night, **Dovercourt House** (ⓐ 805 Dovercourt Rd
🕿 416-535-3847 Ⓦ www.dovercourthouse.com) hosts a
swing dance party with an hour's lesson beforehand. For
comedy, **Yuk Yuks** (ⓐ 224 Richmond St W 🕿 416- 967-6425
Ⓦ www.yukyuks.com) and **Second City** (ⓐ 51 Mercer St
🕿 416-343-0033 Ⓦ www.secondcity.com) have great stand-up
shows, while **Bad Dog Theatre** (ⓐ 138 Danforth Ave 🕿 416-491-3115
Ⓦ www.baddogtheatre.com) offers pure improvised comedy.

Partying takes place at the weekend, with weekdays being
usually quiet. Most public transport stops at 01.30, so things quieten
down then with many revellers trickling back to their lodgings.

Sport & relaxation

Toronto is a hockey town even though the team – the Toronto Maple Leafs – hasn't won the Stanley Cup in decades. Baseball is also increasingly popular. The main stadia in Toronto are the **Air Canada Centre** (ⓐ 40 Bay St ⓣ 416-815-5500 ⓦ www.theaircanadacentre.com), the **Rogers Centre** (ⓐ One Blue Jays Way ⓣ 416-341-3000 ⓦ www.rogerscentre.com) and the **BMO Field** (ⓐ 170 Princes Blvd ⓣ 416-360-4625 ⓦ www.bmofield.com). Tickets for most matches can be obtained through Ticketmaster (see page 28).

SPECTATOR SPORTS

Baseball After taking the **Blue Jays** (ⓦ http://toronto.bluejays. mlb.com) to two World Series in the early 1990s, manager Cito Gaston has returned to lead the team to glory again. Home games take place from early spring to late autumn at the Rogers Centre, with tickets running anywhere from $9 in the nosebleed section to over $200.

Football & soccer The **Argonauts** (ⓦ www.argonauts.ca) football team have been in existence since 1873, boasting 15 Grey Cups wins. The season runs from June to the end of autumn, with home games played at the Rogers Centre; tickets cost $30–80. Toronto FC (ⓦ http://toronto.fc.mlsnet.com) are Canada's first Major League soccer team, playing home games at the BMO Field stadium.

Hockey The **Toronto Maple Leafs** (🅦 http://mapleleafs.nhl.com) play at the Air Canada Centre from autumn to spring. Tickets are notoriously expensive, costing upwards of $100 for a 'cheap' seat.

Basketball The Raptors basketball team has held its own for the last couple of years. Matches take place at the Air Canada Centre in autumn, winter and spring.

Lacrosse Sadly underrated despite recent strong performances, **Toronto Rock** (🅦 www.torontorock.com) play at the Air Canada Centre. Tickets for games, in winter and spring, run from $30–80.

PARTICIPATION SPORTS

Winter is perfect for alpine skiing and winter sports. 90 minutes away by car is **Blue Mountain** (🕿 705-445-0231 🅦 www.bluemountain.ca), the largest ski resort in Ontario. In summer, you can join in volleyball games along Balmy, Kew and Woodbine beaches, or go for an early morning cycle or jog along the Beaches boardwalk in the East End. The **Harbourfront Canoe & Kayak Centre** (🕿 416-203-2277 🅦 www.paddletoronto.com) hires out canoes and kayaks at reasonable rates, and the islands (see page 66) are only a quick paddle away.

RELAXATION

Almost every major hotel in the city has a stellar spa to go with it, with most open to the public. The **Elmwood Spa** (🅐 18 Elm St 🕿 416-977-6751 🅦 www.elmwoodspa.com) is the largest and most elegant of the lot since its multi-million dollar facelift.

ALGONQUIN PROVINCIAL PARK

The oldest park in Ontario is an outdoor-lover's paradise, with 2,000 lakes and 7,725 sq km (2,980 sq miles) of land to explore by foot, bike or canoe.

The **Algonquin Visitor Centre** (📍 43 km (27 miles) past West gate 🌐 www.algonquinpark.on.ca 🕐 09.00–21.00 summer; 10.00–16.00 Sat & Sun, winter) can provide information, but first-time visitors should contact a tour operator such as **Algonquin Outfitters** (📞 1-800-469-4948 🌐 www.algonquinoutfitters.com) or the bespoke **Voyageur Quest** (📞 416-486-3605 🌐 www.voyageurquest.com).

Algonquin is situated about 300 km (186 miles) north of Toronto and is best visited by car. Take Highways 400, 11 then 60 to reach it. **Greyhound buses** (📞 1-800-661-8747 🌐 www.greyhound.ca) also travel daily from Toronto's main bus Terminal to Huntsville, southwest of the park, and Maynooth, where you can hire a canoe and paddle into the park via its southern tip. There are campsites and three lodges with restaurants in the park itself, but make sure you book well in advance (and bring your own beer or wine if you want to drink – serving alcohol inside the park is illegal). The **Portage Store** (📞 705-633-5622 or 705-789-3645 🌐 www.portagestore.com 🕐 07.00–21.00 summer; 08.00–19.00 spring & autumn) serves breakfast, lunch and dinner in its large dining room overlooking Canoe Lake. If you're camping, make sure you bring some marshmallows and indulge in the quintessential Canadian campfire experience of s'mores – melted marshmallows and chocolate chips sandwiched between graham crackers.

On a rainy day, or if you need some recovery time, head to the **Algonquin Logging Museum** (ⓐ East gate ⓛ 09.00–21.00 summer; 10.00–16.00 Sat & Sun, winter), which traces the history of Algonquin park from its beginnings as a logging industry initiative to its present-day protected park status. The **Algonquin Art Centre** (ⓐ Found Lake ⓦ www.algonquinartcentre.com ⓛ 10.00–17.30 summer) offers another handy cultural respite and has a lovely outdoor café.

🔺 *Outdoor sports or pure relaxation at Algonquin Provincial Park*

Accommodation

It seems Toronto travellers like to be pampered, as the city has cultivated a wide selection of upscale boutique hotels. The latest additions to the city's accommodation scene are so-called art gallery hotels like The Drake and The Gladstone, which have live-in artists and music venues as well as bars and restaurants. If cheap, rather than chic, is the aim there's a wide range of bunks and hostels available. Rates fluctuate depending on the day, the season and availability, so check for special offers; booking in advance can cut 10–15 per cent off the standard rate, as can stays of a week or more. When festivals and city-wide events such as TIFF are on (see page 8), book well in advance.

HOTELS

Delta Chelsea Hotel ££–£££ A comfortable hotel with a pool, gym and a balcony in most rooms. **ⓐ** 33 Gerrard St W (Downtown) **ⓣ** 416-595-1975 **ⓦ** www.deltahotels.com **ⓝ** Subway: College, Dundas; streetcar: 506 Carlton

The Drake Hotel ££–£££ In addition to themed rooms and artist-

PRICE CATEGORIES
Price ratings in this guide are based on the average cost of a room for two people per night, not including tax or breakfast.
£ up to $100   ££ $100–200   £££ over $200

● Art installation adorning The Drake Hotel

◆ *The red-brick façade of the Gladstone Hotel*

curated spaces, this uber-hip hotel contains an arts venue, restaurant and bar. ⓐ 1150 Queen St W (West End) ⓣ 416-531-5042 ⓦ www.thedrakehotel.ca Ⓝ Streetcar: 501 Queen

Gladstone Hotel ££–£££ The same art-gallery style vibe as The Drake, but more low-key and community-oriented. ⓐ 1214 Queen St W (West End) ⓣ 416- 531-4635 ⓦ www.gladstonehotel.com Ⓝ Streetcar: 501 Queen; bus: 29 Dufferin

Hazelton Hotel £££ Located in the chi-chi Yorkville area, this swank spot boasts a 5-star status. ⓐ 118 Yorkville Ave (Downtown) ⓣ 416-963-6300 ⓦ www.thehazeltonhotel.com Ⓝ Subway: Bay, St George

Hôtel Le Germain £££ One of the most beautifully designed hotels in Toronto, this spot has a relaxing, well-designed feel. ⓐ 30 Mercer St (Downtown) ⓣ 416-345-9500 ⓦ www.germaintoronto.com Ⓝ Subway: St. Andrew; streetcar: 504 King

Pantages £££ Think clean lines, luxurious linens and martinis in the lounge: this is a place to pamper yourself. ⓐ 200 Victoria St (Downtown) ⓣ 416-945-5444 ⓦ www.pantageshotel.com Ⓝ Subway: Dundas; streetcar: 501 Queen, 505 Dundas

Windsor Arms Hotel £££ All neo-Gothic décor and wood panelling, this lux place has a quaint tea room and deluxe spa attached. ⓐ 18 St Thomas St (Downtown) ⓣ 416-971-9666 ⓦ www.windsorarmshotel.com Ⓝ Subway: Bay

APARTMENTS & GUESTHOUSES

Les Amis Bed & Breakfast ££ If you're picky about food, this B&B in a Victorian townhouse will make sure you eat right in the morning – it specialises in vegetarian breakfasts. ⓐ 31 Granby St (Downtown) ⓣ 416-591-0635 ⓦ www.bbtoronto.com ⓝ Subway: College; streetcar: 506 Carlton

Annex Quest House ££ Equipped with 18 eco-friendly rooms that can accommodate day, week or month-long stays in the relaxed Annex neighbourhood. ⓐ 83 Spadina Rd (Downtown) ⓣ 416-922-1934 ⓦ www.annexquesthouse.com ⓝ Subway: Spadina

Au Petit Paris ££ A unique spin on a homey B&B with its French and vegetarian vibes. ⓐ 3 Selby St (Downtown) ⓣ 416-928-1348 ⓦ www.bbtoronto.com/aupetitparis ⓝ Subway: Sherbourne, Bloor; bus: 75 Sherbourne

A Seaton Dream ££ An up-to-date B&B in the cosy Downtown neighbourhood of Cabbagetown. ⓐ 243 Seaton St (Downtown) ⓣ 416-929-3363 ⓦ www.aseatondream.com ⓝ Streetcar: 506 Carlton, 505 Dundas

HOSTELS

Canadiana Backpackers Inn £ With a free pancake breakfast and friendly vibe, this place really lives up to its Canadiana title ⓐ 42 Widmer St (Downtown) ⓣ 416-598-9090 ⓦ www.canadianalodging.com ⓝ Subway: St. Andrew; streetcar: 501 Queen, 504 King

Clarence Castle £ A clean, tidy hostel on a quiet street near Toronto's Downtown Entertainment District. ⓐ 8 Clarence Square (Downtown) ⓣ 416-260-1221 ⓦ www.clarencecastle.com ⓝ Streetcar: 510 Spadina, 504 King

College Hostel £ One of the best hostels for location: right next door is a stretch of restaurants, bars and cafés in Kensington Market. Rooms are simple, clean and spacious. ⓐ 280 Augusta Ave (Downtown) ⓣ 416-929-4777 ⓦ www.collegehostel.com ⓝ Streetcar: 506 Carlton, 505 Dundas

Global Village Backpackers £ A perfect spot for the partying type, only steps away from King Street's clubbing district and hosting its own dance parties at weekends. ⓐ 460 King St W (Downtown) ⓣ 416-703-8540 ⓦ www.globalbackpackers.com ⓝ Streetcar: 510 Spadina, 504 King

HI Toronto Hostel £ An old standby, but the Hostelling International chain can be depended on for cheap, clean rooms. ⓐ 76 Church St (Downtown) ⓣ 416-971-4440 ⓦ www.hostellingtoronto.com ⓝ Subway: King; streetcar: 504 King

Neill-Wycik Hotel £ Only available from May to August, this student residence transforms into a very affordable place to stay with its open kitchen and shared bathrooms. Not ideal if privacy is desired, but a good way to meet fellow travellers. ⓐ 96 Gerrard St E (Downtown) ⓣ 416-977-2320 ⓦ www.neill-wycik.com ⓝ Subway: College; streetcar: 506 Carlton

THE BEST OF TORONTO

From one of the tallest structures in the world to a castle built by a soon-to-be bankrupted businessman, there are plenty of things to see and do around Toronto.

TOP 10 ATTRACTIONS

- **Casa Loma** Built in 1911 by Sir Henry Pellatt, who eventually went broke and lost ownership of the estate, Toronto's only castle is complete with secret passageways, a library, ball room and gardens (see page 58)

- **Royal Ontario Museum** Almost six million objects are packed into Canada's largest museum (see page 68)

- **Art Gallery of Ontario** Tear your gaze away from the graceful architecture of the AGO, and check out the amazing collections of art on display (see page 66)

- **Hockey Hall of Fame** Hockey lovers will love it in this historic building, which contains a replica of the Montreal Canadiens' dressing room and a simulation zone where you can practise your slap shot (see page 64)

⬇ *View towards Toronto's marina and Downtown*

- **St Lawrence Market** One of the oldest spots in the city, the market has a 200-year history. Now it's Toronto's favourite farmers' market (see page 71)

- **CN Tower** The massive spike that put Toronto on the map. Sure, it's kitschy, but walking on a glass floor suspended 1,122 feet above ground is not something to miss (see page 62)

- **Toronto Islands** The islands, whose residents fended off the city government and received 100-year leases on their cottages, is a peaceful, green spot filled with bike paths, a mini amusement park and plenty of picnic tables (see page 66)

- **Gerrard India Bazaar** Also known as Little India, this stretch of Indian and Pakistani restaurants and shops has some of the best street food in the city (see page 96)

- **High Park** The crown jewel of Toronto's park system, with the historic Colborne Lodge and a mini zoo (see page 80)

- **Kensington Market** This Downtown neighbourhood, with its tightly packed vintage and cheese shops, bakeries and cafés has a lot of charm and plenty to explore (see page 71)

Suggested itineraries

HALF-DAY: TORONTO IN A HURRY

Start the morning or afternoon with a sandwich at St Lawrence Market (see page 71). Walk north to Queen Street East to catch the iconic Queen streetcar, hopping off at Bathurst Street to explore the hip boutiques, record stores and restaurants.

1 DAY: TIME TO SEE A LITTLE MORE

From Union Station, wander north up Bay Street and grab a bite to eat at Nathan Phillips Square (see page 65), where the new and old City Halls stand. Spend time exploring the Distillery District (see page 64), and in the evening head out to the trendy neighbourhood of Parkdale (see page 76) for dinner and cocktails.

2–3 DAYS: TIME TO SEE MUCH MORE

You'll have time to explore Toronto's excellent museums, so buy a CityPass (see page 22) for free access to many of them. Take a trip up the CN Tower (see page 62) and spend an evening in the studenty area of Annex, near Spadina Station, enjoying a relaxed drink and cheap, good nosh.

LONGER: ENJOYING TORONTO TO THE FULL

Lose yourself in Chinatown (see page 62) or the Gerrard India Bazaar (see page 96). Take a day trip out to see the Niagara Falls (see page 111), or enjoy the cultural town of Stratford (see page 118).

◯ Toronto's new City Hall on Nathan Phillips Square

Something for nothing

Toronto's growing number of markets are a great place to find free entertainment, as well as pick up samples of delicious food. The classic St Lawrence Market (see page 71) is open throughout the week, selling veggies, fruit, meat and cheese. On Saturdays in spring and autumn, the Don Valley Brick Works market (yes, on the site of a former brickyard) is the place to find organic food and free samples. Check out ⓦ www.veg.ca for locations of other seasonal markets – all are worth visiting.

The major museums offer free entrance at certain times. The ROM (see page 68), for example, is free between 16.30 and 17.30 on Wednesdays and the AGO (see page 66) is free on Wednesdays between 18.00 and 22.30. You can also browse the private galleries in 401 Richmond (see page 46) for free. If you have kids in tow, take them to **Riverdale Farm** (ⓐ 201 Winchester St ⓣ 416 961-8787 ⓦ www.friendsofriverdalefarm.com ⓛ 09.00–17.00 ⓝ Subway: Castlefrank; streetcar: 506 Carlton), a quaint little park with plenty of meandering paths and farm animals.

In summer, head to the East End's beach boardwalk, crammed with people strolling, picnicking, barbecuing and sunbathing. In the winter months, the city maintains several free ice rinks (check ⓦ www.toronto.ca), although there's a small charge for renting skates.

Evening entertainment doesn't have to be costly either. Toronto's flashy Yonge-Dundas Square, modelled on New York's Times Square, features free music and cultural events almost every weekend – see ⓦ www.ydsquare.ca). The Canadian Broadcasting Company, or **CBC** (ⓣ 1-866-306-4636 ⓦ www.cbc.ca) hands out free tickets to its live shows, including 'The Hour' and the comedic Rick Mercer Report. Classical music lovers under 30 can get tickets to see the Canadian Opera Company (see page 18) for just $20 – but only 150 such tickets are offered for each performance so get hold of it well in advance.

⬥ Skating for free in a public ice rink in Nathan Phillips Square

When it rains

Feel a few drops coming on? If it's just a short shower, head to one of Toronto's excellent cafés until it passes, such as MoRoCo (see page 72) in Downtown's Yorkville district or the French Clafouti bakery (see page 86) on Queen Street West. A rainy afternoon or evening can be spent drinking and nibbling in one of the city's growing number of tapas lounges.

If it's more of a deluge that's threatening to ruin the day, head for one of the major museums such as the Royal Ontario Museum (see page 68) or Art Gallery of Ontario (see page 66) – you could easily spend a whole morning or even a day admiring the works on display there, and the AGO has a cosy cinematheque with a great programme of classic and obscure films. Another cultural alternative is **401 Richmond** (ⓐ 401 Richmond St W ① 416-595-5900 Ⓦ www.401richmond.net Ⓝ Streetcar: 501 Queen, 510 Spadina), an art centre inside an old tin lithography factory which now contains over 140 businesses including studios and galleries. The insides are all exposed brick and hardwood floors, with a few catwalks that give a good view of the building and courtyard. There's an excellent café on the bottom floor and, if the weather clears up, you can check out the rooftop garden and its experiments in vertical gardening.

If you're not really into museums or just fancy some light entertainment, head to the microbrewer Mill Street Brewery in the Distillery District (see page 64) or to the **Steam Whistle Brewery** (ⓐ 255 Bremner Blvd ① 416-362-2337 Ⓦ www.steamwhistle.ca ● 12.00–18.00 Mon–Sat, 12.00–17.00 Sun Ⓝ Subway: Union;

streetcar: 510 Spadina), Toronto's largest beer brewer. Both offer tours and tastings.

⬤ *Frank Gehry's unique spiral staircase in the Art Gallery of Ontario*

On arrival

TIME DIFFERENCE

Toronto follows Eastern Standard Time (EST), five hours behind Greenwich Mean Time (GMT). From March to November, the clock is set forward one hour for Daylight Saving Time.

ARRIVING

By air

International flights arrive at **Toronto Pearson International Airport** (❶ 1-866-207-1690 ⓦ www.gtaa.com), approximately 32 km (20 miles) from Downtown. It has all the usual facilities, plus free Wi-Fi internet. A tourist information booth is located in Terminal 3.

The 192 Airport Rocket shuttle bus travels to Kipling subway station every 10–15 minutes between 05.20–02.00, taking around 20 minutes and costing $2.75 one way at the time of writing. Between 02.00–05.00, the 300A night bus runs from the airport to Danforth Avenue and Bloor Street while the 307 goes to Yonge Street and Eglington Avenue. If you have lots of bags, you may prefer to take a cab or a smarter limo taxi – the latter are often more convenient and cheaper, with flat rates based on the destination. The taxi rank is just outside the airport, and limos can be booked in advance from **Toronto Airport Limousine** (❶ 416-836-0450 ⓦ www.limoairporttoronto.com) or **Aeroport Taxi & Limousine** (❶ 905-908-5000 ⓦ www.aeroporttaxi.com). Expect to pay at least $50 for a journey into the city, and beware that travelling in rush hour can delay you by an hour or more.

Toronto City Centre Airport (a 60 Harbour St t 416-203-6942 w www.torontoport.com) on Toronto Islands receives flights from other Canadian and North American cities. The airport is small and relaxing, with free Wi-Fi and complimentary drinks for departing passengers. A ferry transfers passengers every ten minutes from the airport to the southern tip of Bathurst Street, from where travellers can catch a frequent, free bus shuttle to the Downtown core. Alternatively, the 511 Bathurst streetcar runs to Bathurst Station and the 509 Harbourfront streetcar goes to Union Station.

◆ *Spectacular walkway at Union Station*

Toronto

0 2000 metres
0 2000 yards

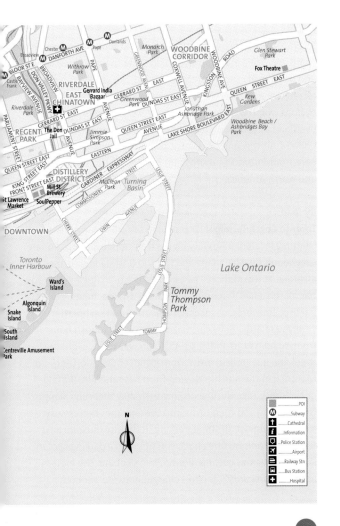

By rail

Toronto's central railway station is **Union Station** (ⓐ 65 Front St W ⓣ 416-366-7788) in Downtown, which links to the subway network and has a ready supply of taxis outside. The station is almost an attraction in itself, with its gleaming marble floors and vaulted ceilings, and the view of Front Street's skyscrapers looming overhead as you emerge from the train is dramatic. VIA Rail Canada, Amtrak and GO Transit trains (see page 128) all arrive here from Toronto's suburbs and from other cities in Canada and North America.

By road

Toronto Coach Terminal (ⓐ 610 Bay St ⓣ 416-393-7911) is centrally located only a few blocks from Yonge-Dundas Square. Greyhound, Coach Canada and Ontario Northland coach services all arrive at this station. The terminal is a manageable size and has all the usual amenities, including ATM machines, lockers, parking, free internet access and an information booth.

If you're arriving by car, make sure you avoid rush hour, from 06.30–09.30 and 15.30–18.30 on weekdays. Highways 401 (free) and 407 (tolled) arrive from Windsor, Ontario, Detroit or Montreal in the north. If driving from Niagara Falls, Buffalo or New York, take the Queen Elizabeth Way that runs along Lake Ontario and then turns into the Gardiner Expressway. Note that almost all street parking in the city must be paid for at electronic meters on pavements, with a parking spot in Downtown areas costing around $1–3 per hour. The meters accept credit cards. Car parks charge up to $10 per hour.

ON YER BIKE

Cycling in Toronto is safe and often quicker than public transport or a taxi. **Community Bicycle Network** (ⓐ 761 Queen St W ❶ 416-504-2918 ⓦ www.communitybicyclenetwork.org) offer good-value bicycle rental. The **Bike Train** initiative (ⓦ www.biketrain.ca) allows you to take bikes on major train routes. Lights are obligatory when cycling at night, and all bicycles must have a bell.

FINDING YOUR FEET

Toronto's pace during the rush hour is near frantic, but at other times the atmosphere is relaxed. It is relatively safe, but at night try to avoid the area around Lansdowne Station, the stretch along Queen Street East between Church Street and Sherbourne, and Moss Park.

ORIENTATION

Toronto is easy to navigate. The CN Tower (see page 62) is south central and can be seen from almost anywhere in the city. The main highways are the Gardiner Expressway, which cuts the lake off from the city and runs east-west, and the Don Valley Parkway, which follows the valley northwards from the lake. The city is laid out along a grid, with the main arteries University Avenue, Yonge Street, Spadina and Bathurst running north to south and Bloor Street, Queen and King crossing them from east to west.

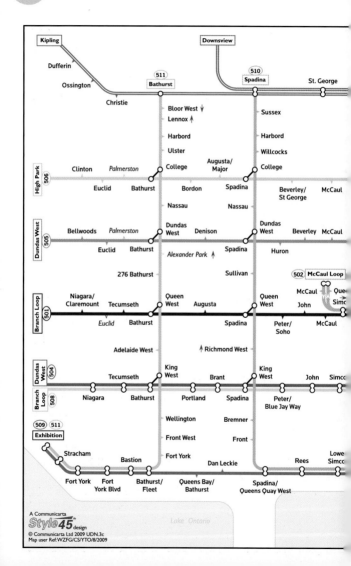

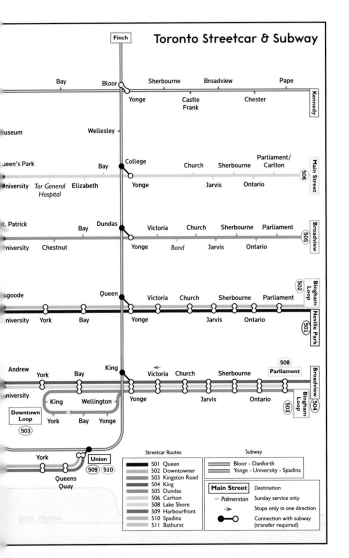

Toronto Streetcar & Subway

Finch

Bloor — Bay — Sherbourne — Broadview — Pape
Yonge — Castle Frank — Chester — Kennedy

Museum — Wellesley

Queen's Park — Bay — College — Church — Sherbourne — Parliament/Carlton
University — Tor General Hospital — Elizabeth — Yonge — Jarvis — Ontario — 506 Main Street

St. Patrick — Bay — Dundas — Victoria — Church — Sherbourne — Parliament
University — Chestnut — Yonge — Bond — Jarvis — Ontario — 505 Broadview

Osgoode — Queen — Victoria — Church — Sherbourne — Parliament — 502 Bingham Loop
University — York — Bay — Yonge — Jarvis — Ontario — 501 Neville Park

St. Andrew — York — Bay — King — Victoria — Church — Sherbourne — 508 Parliament
University — King — Wellington — Yonge — Jarvis — Ontario — 504 Broadview / 503 Bingham Loop

Downtown Loop 503 — York — Bay — Yonge

York — Union 509 510
Queens Quay

Inner Harbour

Streetcar Routes

501 Queen
502 Downtowner
503 Kingston Road
504 King
505 Dundas
506 Carlton
508 Lake Shore
509 Harbourfront
510 Spadina
511 Bathurst

Subway

Bloor – Danforth
Yonge - University - Spadina

Main Street — Destination
Palmerston — Sunday service only
→ — Stops only in one direction
●—○ — Connection with subway (transfer required)

GETTING AROUND

The Toronto Transit Commission, or **TTC** (🌐 www3.ttc.ca) runs all public transport in the city, which consists of two subway (metro) lines, streetcars (trams) and buses. A one-way fare to anywhere in the city on any system costs $2.75 at the time of writing. The subway is the quickest way to get around, using the Yonge–University–Spadina line for north-south transit and Bloor–Danforth for east-west. Streetcars and buses can be slightly more confusing but will get you closer to your destination.

The subway operates from 06.00–01.30 Monday to Saturday and 09.00–01.30 on Sundays, and most buses and streetcars also operate during these times. Queen, King, Bathurst and Carlton streetcars run 24 hours a day and there are several 24-hour and night buses.

Taxis are plentiful in Toronto. Look out for the orange/green **Beck Taxi** (☎ 416-751-5555) and the orange/black **Diamond Taxi** (☎ 416-366-6868) cabs, but there are plenty of smaller reputable companies operating. Taxis are metered, with an off-peak journey costing around $4 plus $0.25 a minute thereafter.

CAR HIRE

You don't need a car to visit places in Toronto, but it may be useful for day trips further afield. **Budget** (🌐 www.budget.com) and **Hertz** (🌐 www.hertz.ca) are two dependable car rental companies with offices at both the airport and in town. In the Downtown area, you can also try **Discount** (📍 730 Yonge St ☎ 416-921-1212 🌐 www.discountcar.com).

◐ *Aerial view of Toronto's Downtown towers*

THE CITY OF
Toronto

Downtown

Toronto's Downtown is where all the action is. Millions of dollars course through the financial district around Bay and King every day. Some of the best theatres, clubs and shops in the country are found here. It might be hard to see now with all the gleaming new skyscrapers, but it was in fact here, on the eastern edge of Downtown, that the city was born in 1834 as a humble community known as York. As you stroll the area, taking in the newer attractions, keep a eye out for the Toronto Heritage plaques on buildings that tell stories about the city's history. Some of the older buildings still remain, like the Flatiron Building at no. 49 Wellington Street East, the Bank of Canada building at no. 252 Adelaide Street East, and St James Cathedral at no. 65 Church Street. The main attractions are conveniently clustered together in a walkable area which is well served by the subway's Yonge-University line.

SIGHTS & ATTRACTIONS

Casa Loma

Built by the eccentric businessman Sir Henry Pellatt in 1914, this dream castle took three years, 300 men and $3.5 million to build (an exorbitant amount at the time). And Casa Loma is certainly everything one would expect from a castle. There are two secret passageways in the study, 22 fireplaces, two towers, stables connected to the castle by a long tunnel and 59 telephones, which at the time handled more calls than the entire city of Toronto. Pellatt eventually fell into debt and was forced to auction off his beloved Casa Loma. ⓐ 1 Austin Terrace, just north

🔺 *Toronto's very own castle, Casa Loma*

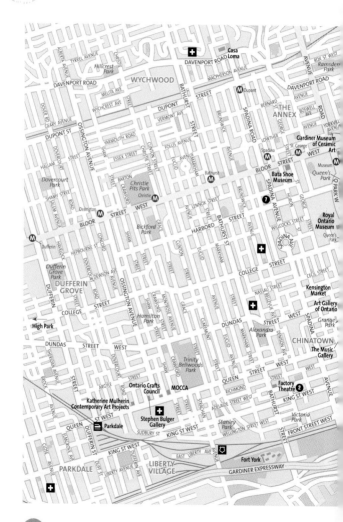

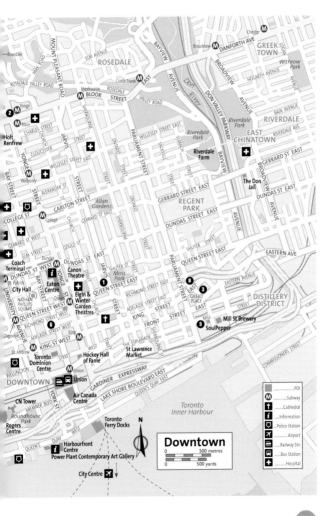

Downtown

0   500 metres

0   500 yards

POI
Subway
Cathedral
Information
Police Station
Airport
Railway Stn
Bus Station
Hospital

THE CITY

of Bloor St ☎ 416-923-1171 ⓦ www.casaloma.org ⏱ 09.30–17.00
(last admission 16.00) Ⓝ Subway: Spadina, St. Clair West; bus:
26 Dupont, 127 Davenport, 7 Bathurst. Admission charge

Chinatown

One of the largest Chinatowns in North America, this district
functions as one huge, chaotic marketplace. Vegetable and
fruit stalls spill onto the sidewalk, as do juice stands and
merchandisers selling cheap watches, jewellery and calling
cards. Wander around, soaking up the atmosphere and poking
inside the cheap clothing stores selling bright kimonos, flip-
flops and fans. Dim sum is the pick-me-up of choice around
here: try **Bright Pearl** (ⓐ 346 Spadina Ave ☎ 416-979-1103
ⓦ www.brightpearlseafood.com ⏱ 09.00–23.00) or the hole-
in-the-wall **Mother's Dumplings** (ⓐ 79 Huron St, off Dundas St W
☎ 416-217-2008 ⓦ www.mothersdumplings.com ⏱ 11.00–23.00).
Ⓝ Streetcar: 510 Spadina, 501 Queen, 505 Dundas

CN Tower

Built during the prosperous 1970s, the CN Tower was a potent
symbol of Canadian ambition. From 1976 to 2007 it held the
record for being the tallest freestanding structure in the world
at 553 m (1,815) ft. Inside, visitors ride a glass-walled elevator up
to the observation deck, where there's a glass floor – a trip that's
probably best avoided if you suffer from vertigo. ⓐ 301 Front St W
☎ 416-868-6937 ⓦ www.cntower.ca ⏱ 09.00–23.00 Ⓝ Subway:
Union. Admission charge

⏵ *CN Tower alongside the oval of the Rogers Centre*

Distillery District

This must be the only district in the world with a single street address – due to the fact that the entire 'district' is contained within the grounds of an old whisky factory. The 13 red brick streets and 44 historic buildings of this newly chic area belonged to the old Gooderham and Worts Distillery that churned out whisky way back in the 1800s, and are some of Canada's finest examples of Victorian-era industrial architecture. Newly revamped after years of neglect, they're now home to gourmet food shops, bakeries, cafés, art galleries and design shops. It's fun to explore the area on your own, but to get an idea of the history behind the place you can book an hour-long **guided tour** (☎ 1-866-405-8687 ⏱ 11.30–15.30 Tues–Sun). If beer's more your tipple than whisky, pay a trip to the **Mill Street Brewery** (☎ 416-681-0338 ⓦ www.millstreetbrewery.com), which brews a variety of organic ales. ⓐ 55 Mill St ☎ 416-364-1177 ⓦ www.thedistillerydistrict.com ⏱ 24 hrs ⓝ Streetcar: 504 King, 501 Queen

Fort York

Fort York was built by Ontario's first Lieutenant Governor in 1793 as protection against an expected American attack that eventually occurred in the war of 1812. Today, it houses a museum dedicated to this time period. ⓐ 100 Garrison Rd ☎ 416-392-6907 ⓦ www.fortyork.ca ⏱ 10.00–17.00 summer; 10.00–16.00 Mon–Fri, 10.00–17.00 Sat & Sun, winter ⓝ Streetcar: 511 Bathurst. Admission charge

Hockey Hall of Fame

After its unsure beginnings in the 1940s, the Hockey Hall of Fame has became one of the premier sport shrines in the world. The Hall's greatest claim to fame? Home of the Stanley Cup. As well as touring the hockey memorabilia on display, you can take shots at real-time goalies and view some of the greatest ever hockey goals in the two movie theatres. ⓐ 30 Yonge St ⓣ 416-360-7735 ⓦ www.hhof.com ⓛ 09.30–18.00 Mon–Sat, 10.00–18.00 Sun, summer 10.00–17.00 Mon–Fri, 09.30–18.00 Sat, 10.30–17.00 Sun, winter ⓝ Subway: Union. Admission charge

Nathan Phillips Square

Home to the new City Hall and, during the winter, a skating rink. Tours of City Hall are dependent on the availability of security staff so call ahead to fix a time. Crowds flock to the square on New Year's Eve to enjoy the celebratory concert and countdown to midnight. **City Hall** ⓐ 100 Queen St W ⓣ 416-338-0338 ⓦ www.toronto.ca ⓝ Subway: Osgoode, Queen

Rogers Centre

The Rogers Centre (see page 30) is home to both the city's baseball team, the Blue Jays, and the football team, the Argonauts. Don't worry if the weather turns wet, as the stadium just closes its snazzy retractable roof. One-hour tours of the stadium, the luxury suites and the Blue Jays Hall of Fame run daily but tour times vary depending on match times; call for details. ⓐ One Blue Jays Way ⓣ 416-341-2770 ⓦ www.rogerscentre.com. Admission charge

Toronto Dominion Centre

This black-lined building by Mies van der Rohe is best seen at night, when the hundreds of lighted windows are gorgeous against

the sky. @ 66 Wellington St W ☎ 416-869-1144 🌐 www.tdcentre.ca
🕐 08.30–16.30 Mon–Fri Ⓝ Subway: Union, King, St. Andrew;
streetcar: 504 King

Toronto Islands

Built on sand-bars that stretch out into the bay, it's surprising
how faraway these little islands feel: a much slower pace, no
cars, only cyclists, walkers, cleaner air and the best view of the
city. Catch the ferry from the Toronto Ferry Docks at the foot of
Bay Street to one of the three main islands – Hanlan's Point,
Ward's Island and Centre Island. All three are interconnected
by walkways and bike paths, so it's easy to get from one to
another. Hanlan's Point has two supervised beaches as well as
an infamous 'clothing optional' beach, while Ward's Island and
its little neighbour Algonquin Island are mainly residential, filled
with tiny cottages clustered along a network of paved paths.
On Centre Island you'll find the **Centreville Amusement Park**
(☎ 416-203-0405 🌐 www.centreisland.ca 🕐 10.30–20.00 July
& Aug; 10.30–18.00 May, June & Sept. Admission charge),
an old-fashioned amusement park with a winding mini-train
and twirling teacup ride. **Toronto Ferry Docks** @ Queen's Quay
☎ 416-392-8193 🌐 www.toronto.ca/parks/island 🕐 Ferries
depart every 30–45 mins; times vary according to island
& season Ⓝ Subway: Union ❶ Reduced schedule in winter

CULTURE

Art Gallery of Ontario

Toronto's newly revamped art gallery touts the work of big

Canadian artists like Greg Curnoe and Michael Snow. Inside, you'll find the Cinematheque, which offers an eclectic programme of old, experimental, obscure and classic films. ⓐ 317 Dundas St W ⓣ 416-979-6648 ⓦ www.ago.net & www.cinemathequeontario.ca ⓛ 10.00–17.30 Tues, Thur–Sun, 10.00–22.30 Wed ⓝ Subway: St. Patrick; streetcar: 505 Dundas, 501 Queen. Admission charge

Bata Shoe Museum

Shoe fanatics can gaze in awe and jealousy at Sonja Bata's personal collection of shoes from around the world, including a pair made of human hair and a pair of John Lennon's Beatle boots. Her collection is suitably enshrined in a sleek building in Downtown. ⓐ 327 Bloor St W ⓣ 416-979-7799 ⓦ www.batashoemuseum.ca ⓛ 10.00–17.00 Mon–Wed, Fri & Sat, 10.00–20.00 Thur, 12.00–17.00 Sun. Admission charge

Fleck Dance Theatre

Based in the huge Harbourfront Centre arts complex, this theatre hosts the country's top dance companies as well as several diverse dance festivals throughout the year. The CanAsian International Dance Festival (ⓦ www.canasiandancefestival.com) in May is one to look out for. ⓐ 207 Queens Quay West ⓣ 416-973-4600 ⓦ www.harbourfrontcentre.com ⓝ Subway: Union; streetcar: 504 King

Gardiner Museum of Ceramic Art

It doesn't have the big names of Libeskind or Gehry attached, but the clean lines of the Gardiner building, and its collection of ceramics, are beloved by the city. ⓐ 111 Queen's Park

416-586-8080 www.gardinermuseum.on.ca Subway: Museum. Admission charge

The Music Gallery
Currently located inside the St George the Martyr Anglican Church, this hub for experimental music has existed in various buildings across the city for over thirty years. Concert tickets are available online or from Soundscapes (see page 84).
197 John St 416-204-1080 www.musicgallery.org
Subway: Osgoode; streetcar: 501 Queen

Power Plant Contemporary Art Gallery
A public gallery that puts on cutting-edge art shows which are occasionally mystifying but always impressive. Part of the Harbourfront Centre, the Power Plant features both rising and renowned artists from Canada and around the world. 231 Queens Quay West 416-973-4949
www.thepowerplant.org 12.00–18.00 Tues–Sun, 12.00–20.00 Wed Subway: Union; streetcar: 504 King. Admission charge; some events free in summer

Royal Ontario Museum
The country's premier museum, the ROM now has a huge spiky steel addition designed by Daniel Libeskind (see page 20) that has allowed for an extra 100,000 square feet of space and ten new galleries. 100 Queen's Park 416-586-8000
www.rom.on.ca 10.00–17.30 Sat–Thur, 10.00–21.30 Fri
Subway: Museum. Admission charge

◗ *Libeskind's eclectic steel add-on to the Royal Ontario Museum*

RETAIL THERAPY

Independent shops are scattered all over the Distillery District (see page 64). Yorkville is the area to browse if you're after haute couture, trendy boutiques and glitzy accessories.

Eaton Centre All the standard chain shops are here, but the real attraction lies in the fabulous building. It was modelled on Milan's Galleria Vittorio Emanuele, with a huge, open skylight stretching over the shops inside. Acclaimed Canadian artist Michael Snow has installed a mock flock of Canadian geese descending from the open sky above. ⓐ 220 Yonge St ❶ 416-598-8560 ⓦ www.torontoeatoncentre.com ❶ 10.00–21.00 Mon–Fri, 09.30–19.00 Sat, 11.00–18.00 Sun ⓝ Subway: Dundas, Queen; streetcar: 505 Dundas, 501 Queen

Holt Renfrew You can't miss the huge and imposing façade of this haute couture mall at Bay and Bloor. ⓐ 50 Bloor St W ❶ 416-922-2333 ⓦ www.holtrenfrew.com ❶ 10.00–18.00 Mon–Wed, 10.00–20.00 Thur & Fri, 10.00–19.00 Sat, 12.00–18.00 Sun ⓝ Subway: Bay, Bloor

Hudson Bay Company Canada's oldest retail company, which used to trade furs and pelts along Hudson Bay, still sells the signature green, red, yellow and blue blanket that can be found in every Canadian cottage. There is another location at 44 Bloor Street East. ⓐ 176 Yonge St ❶ 416-861-9111 ⓦ www.hbc.com ❶ 10.00–21.00 Mon–Fri, 09.30–19.00 Sat, 11.00–18.00 Sun ⓝ Subway: Queen

Model Citizen Funky selection of men's tie clips, fedoras and shirts. 279 Augusta Ave 416-703-7625 11.00–18.00 Streetcar: 510 Spadina, 506 Carlton, 501 Queen, 505 Dundas

DOWNTOWN MARKETS

Not your average market, **Kensington Market** (www.kensington-market.ca Streetcar: 510 Spadina, 506 Carlton, 501 Queen, 505 Dundas) refers to a boisterous cluster of streets in the middle of Chinatown, a mishmash of different communities and home to ageing hippies, roaming packs of punks and all the other colourful cross-sections of the city. Some of Toronto's most interesting independent shops are located here, including the long-standing bookshop **This Ain't the Rosedale Library** (86 Nassau St 416-929-9912 www.thisaint.ca 11.00–20.00 Mon–Wed, 10.00–22.00 Thur–Sat, 10.00–18.00 Sun) and **Courage My Love** (14 Kensington Ave 416-979-1992 www.peanutbreath.com/courage 11.30–18.00 Mon–Fri, 11.00–18.00 Sat, 13.00–17.00 Sun), a shop that's been selling beads, scarves, vintage prom dresses and other odds and ends for nearly 35 years.

If an average market is what you want, however, head to **St Lawrence Market** (95 Front St E 416-203-2472 www.stlawrencemarket.com 08.00–18.00 Tues–Thur, 08.00–19.00 Fri, 05.00–17.00 Sat & Sun Subway: Union; streetcar: 504 King). Fresh produce and picnic items are on sale during the week, with an antiques fair over on Sundays.

TAKING A BREAK

B Espresso Bar £ ❶ This café is often packed with media professionals from the upstairs offices having a break at the long marble tables. **ⓐ** 111 Queen St E **ⓣ** 416-866-2111 **ⓦ** www.bespressobar.com **ⓛ** 07.30–17.00 Mon–Fri (occasionally 10.00–15.00 Sat & Sun) **Ⓝ** Subway: Queen; streetcar: 501 Queen

Craft Burger £ ❷ Taking its name from its handcrafted burgers, these two burger shops make an excellent blue cheese burger with homemade onion rings. **ⓐ** 573 King St W, 830 Yonge St **ⓣ** 416-596-6660, 416-922-8585 **ⓦ** www.craftburger.com **ⓛ** 11.00–22.00 Mon–Thur, 11.00–23.00 Fri, 12.00–23.00 Sat, 12.00–21.00 Sun **Ⓝ** Subway: St. Andrew, King; streetcar: 504 King

Gilead Café £ ❸ Chef Jamie Kennedy owns this sit-down café on a lane off King Street. The smell of baking bread is irresistible. **ⓐ** 4 Gilead Place **ⓣ** 647-288-0680 **ⓦ** www.gileadcafe.ca **ⓛ** 08.00–18.00 Mon–Wed, Fri, 08.00–17.00 Thur, 08.00–04.00 Sat & Sun **Ⓝ** Subway: King; streetcar: 504 King

MoRoCo £ ❹ A super hideaway in Yorkville, with its chocolate fountain, fondue and truffles amid an Alice-in-Wonderland-style décor. **ⓐ** 99 Yorkville Ave **ⓣ** 416-961-2202 **ⓦ** www.morocochocolat.com **ⓛ** 11.00–22.00 Tues & Wed, 11.00–00.00 Thur–Sat, 11.00–18.00 Sun **Ⓝ** Subway: Bloor, Bay

Soma Chocolatemaker £ ❺ This place just might make the best chocolate in the city – try the creamy melted hot chocolate, truffles

or gelato made in Soma's gelato lab. ❸ 55 Mill St, Building 48
🛈 416-815-7662 🌐 www.somachocolate.com 🕓 10.00–20.00
Mon–Thur, 11.00–21.00 Fri & Sat, 11.00–18.00 Sun (winter hours
vary) Ⓝ Subway: King; streetcar: 504 King

AFTER DARK

RESTAURANTS

Smoke's Poutinerie £ ❻ A joke on Canadiana, this club-district
poutine shop features such wildly inauthentic takes on the country's
national dish as nacho or curried chicken *poutine*. ❸ 218 Adelaide
St W 🛈 416-599-2873 🌐 www.smokespoutinerie.com 🕓 11.30–23.00
Mon–Wed, 11.30–03.00 Thur & Fri, 11.30–04.00 Sat, 11.30–21.00
Sun Ⓝ Subway: St. Andrew; streetcar: 504 King, 501 Queen

The Harbord Room ££ ❼ Harbord Street is becoming a
culinary destination, but this restaurant stands out from the
rest with simple but excellent continental food. ❸ 89 Harbord St
🛈 416-962-8989 🌐 www.theharbordroom.com 🕓 18.00–22.30
Mon–Sat; 10.30–14.00, 18.00–22.30 Sun Ⓝ Subway: Spadina;
streetcar: 510 Spadina; bus: 94 Wellesley

Weezie's ££ ❽ A quiet, tasteful bistro that serves excellent
continental fare. ❸ 354 King St E 🛈 416-777-9339 🕓 17.30–22.00
Tues–Sat Ⓝ Streetcar: 504 King, 501 Queen; bus: 65 Parliament

BARS & CLUBS

BarChef One of the best places to drink fancy (and pricey)
cocktails before a big night out. Look to the special Recession

menu for cheaper selections. ⓐ 472 Queen St W ⓣ 416-868-4800 ⓦ www.barcheftoronto.com ⓛ 17.30–02.00 Tues–Fri, 20.00–02.00 Sat ⓝ Streetcar: 501 Queen, 511 Bathurst, 510 Spadina

Dominion on Queen This hotel from the 1800s has been converted into a bar with a pool table, a jazz show most nights and 16 beers on tap. ⓐ 500 Queen St E ⓣ 416-368-6893 ⓦ www.dominiononqueen.com ⓛ 11.00–01.00 Mon–Sat, 11.00–23.00 Sun ⓝ Subway: Queen; streetcar: 501 Queen, 504 King

Lee's Palace One of the city's longest-running rock clubs, Lee's downstairs venue is a treat: great acoustics, seating and tables around the edges as well as a dance floor and a bar in the back. Upstairs, the Dance Cave is where university students get down. ⓐ 529 Bloor St W ⓣ 416-532-1598 ⓦ www.leespalace.com ⓛ Until 03.00; hours vary according to event ⓝ Subway: Bathurst, Spadina

Pantages Martini Bar The best Happy Hour in the city, with excellent $5 martinis served in a swanky hotel lounge. ⓐ 200 Victoria St ⓣ 416-945-5444 ⓦ www.pantageshotel.com ⓛ 16.00–00.00 Sun–Thur, 16.00–01.00 Fri & Sat ⓝ Subway: Queen; streetcar: 501 Queen

The Pilot Tavern One of the few left-over pubs from Yorkville's edgier days, The Pilot has a decidedly laid-back feel. Expect jazz at weekends and a packed roof patio in the summer. ⓐ 22 Cumberland St ⓣ 416-923-5716 ⓦ www.thepilot.ca ⓛ 11.30–01.00 Mon & Tues, 11.30–02.00 Wed–Fri, 12.30–02.00 Sat, 12.00–22.00 Sun ⓝ Subway: Bloor, Bay

◆ *Try the various beers on tap at Dominion on Queen*

West End

After hours, the West End is the place to be. The pick of the city's concert venues, bars and restaurants are here; be sure to check out what's on at the arty Drake and Gladstone hotels (see pages 34 & 37) in particular. This end of town is more condensed than other areas, with many of the hang-outs and party places concentrated along Dundas Street and Queen Street West.

It's worth exploring the other neighbourhoods, though, which all have a distinctive character. Parkdale, which starts after Gladstone Avenue along Queen Street West and ends at Roncesvalles, is becoming increasingly popular with young, creative professionals and their kids. Bistros and brunch spots are popping up all over this newly trendy area. Liberty Village, the stretch below King Street West between Niagara and Dufferin, has a more gentrified Brooklyn feel to it. Most of the streets are filled with warehouses that have now been taken over by creative businesses. The Junction, which begins at Dundas West and curls upwards towards Keele Street, is slowly recruiting fans with its live music bars and growing selection of restaurants and cafés – it's just on the verge of catching up with hot 'hoods like Parkdale, so visit before the crowds arrive.

SIGHTS & ATTRACTIONS

Dufferin Grove Park

Just when Dufferin starts to feel congested with traffic, this West End park offers some much-needed greenery. Local residents have transformed the park in the last few years with a garden,

⬤ *Dufferin Grove Park is a peaceful oasis in the West End of the city*

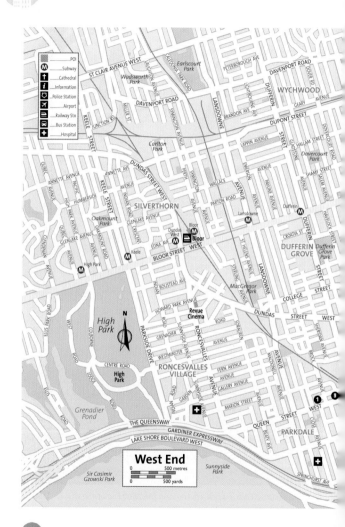

farmers' market, summer wading pool and – strange but true – communal pizza oven. 'Pizza days' are held 13.00–15.00 Sundays and 12.00–14.00 Wednesdays at a cost of $2.50 per person, with a community supper ($6) at 18.00 on Fridays. ⓐ 875 Dufferin St ⓣ 416-392-0913 ⓦ www.toronto.ca/parks ⓛ 24 hrs; market: 15.00–19.00 Thur ⓢ Subway: Dufferin; bus: 29 Dufferin; streetcar: 506 Carlton

High Park

A natural, free-flowing park with over a third of its grounds in a natural state and the rest filled with attractions such as the cultivated Hillside Gardens, Grenadier Pond, a trackless train that weaves through the park during the warmer months and a small zoo. In the winter, locals cross-country ski through the park. Near the south entrance is Colborne Lodge, an historic 1837 cottage furnished with period furniture. ⓐ 1873 Bloor St W ⓣ Park: 416-392-1111; lodge: 416-392-6916 ⓛ Park: 24 hrs; lodge: 12.00–16.00 Fri–Sun, mid-Jan, Feb, April; 12.00–16.00 Thur–Sun, Mar; 12.00–17.00 Tues–Sun, May–Aug; 12.00–17.00 Sat & Sun, Sept; 12.00–16.00 Tues–Sun, Oct–Dec ⓢ Subway: Keele, High Park, Runnymede; streetcar: 505 Dundas, 506 Carlton

Trinity Bellwoods Park

Queen Street West's beautiful park, with a valley, tennis court, farmers' market and scattered picnic tables. On a sunny day, the park is filled with picnickers, sunbathers and people sneakily taking swigs of beer (drinking in open public spaces is illegal in Canada so watch out). Look for the unique pair of white squirrels who are resident here. ⓐ 1053 Dundas St W ⓣ 416-392-1111

◢ *A local art fair in Trinity Bellwoods Park*

Ⓦ www.toronto.ca/parks ⏱ 24 hrs; market: 15.00–19.00 Tues
Ⓝ Streetcar: 501 Queen, 505 Dundas

CULTURE

Katherine Mulherin Contemporary Art Projects

The queen bee of any Queen West gallery walk, this trio of
galleries was named after its groundbreaking owner and
curator, who is often credited with transforming this area
into a gallery district. ⓐ 1080, 1082 & 1086 Queen St West

MUSEUM OF CONTEMPORARY CANADIAN ART (MOCCA)

Entirely devoted to Canadian art, this gallery museum contains around 400 works by over 150 artists. Temporary exhibitions feature the works of well-known personalities such as industrial landscape photographer Edward Burtynsky. The shop sells books related to the museum's research projects. ⓐ 952 Queen St W ⓣ 416-395-0067 ⓦ www.mocca.ca ⓛ 11.00–18.00 Tues–Thur, Sat & Sun 11.00–21.00 Fri ⓝ Streetcar: 501 Queen; bus: 63 Ossington. Admission by donation

ⓣ 416-993-6510 ⓦ www.katharinemulherin.com ⓛ Hours vary ⓝ Streetcar: 501 Queen; bus: 63 Ossington

Ontario Crafts Council

A little non-profit gallery which displays arts and crafts of all different types: hand-stitched notebooks, cutesy dolls, magnets and sometimes even a full-scale art installation. ⓐ 990 Queen St W ⓣ 416-925-4222 ⓦ www.craft.on.ca ⓛ 11.00–17.00 Tues–Fri, 11.00–18.00 Sat, 12.00–17.00 Sun ⓝ Streetcar: 501 Queen, bus: 63 Ossington

Stephen Bulger Gallery

A clean, almost minimalist gallery with exhibitions of modern photography as well as historical photographs rescued from bygone eras. The adjoining bar and theatre, **Camera** (ⓣ 416-530-0011

Ⓦ www.camerabar.ca) screens art-house films on Saturdays at 13.00.
Ⓐ 1026 Queen St W Ⓣ 416-504-0575 Ⓦ www.bulgergallery.com
Ⓛ 11.00–18.00 Tues–Sat Ⓝ Streetcar: 501 Queen; bus: 63 Ossington

RETAIL THERAPY

69 Vintage An emporium of vintage clothes, including
tailored suits, perfectly scuffed cowboy boots and sweeping
ballroom gowns. Ⓐ 1100 Queen St W Ⓣ 416-516-0669
Ⓦ www.69vintage.com Ⓛ 12.00–19.00 Ⓝ Streetcar: 501 Queen;
bus: 63 Ossington, 29 Dufferin

Cabaret A shop which prides itself on selling absolutely pristine
vintage goods, such as perfectly preserved top hats and bowlers,
Jackie O style dresses and leather mantels. Ⓐ 672 Queen St W
Ⓣ 416-504-7126 Ⓦ www.cabaretvintage.com Ⓛ 11.00–18.00
Mon–Wed, Sat, 11.00–19.00 Thur & Fri, 13.00–17.00 Sun
Ⓝ Streetcar: 501 Queen, 511 Bathurst

Carte Blanche An uber-slick store that deals in slinky black leggings,
skinny jeans and stretch satin dresses for women. Ⓐ 758 Queen
St W Ⓣ 416-532-0347 Ⓦ www.shopcarteblanche.ca Ⓛ 11.00–19.00
Mon–Sat, 12.00–18.00 Sun Ⓝ Streetcar: 501 Queen, 511 Bathurst

Franny Vintage Don't be deceived by the exterior of this hole-in-
the wall vintage shop; there are plenty of print dresses, ornamented
belts and bejewelled loafers to go around. Ⓐ 1394 Queen St W
Ⓣ 416-531-8892 Ⓛ 12.00–18.30 Tues–Sat, 12.00–17.00 Sun
Ⓝ Streetcar: 501 Queen; bus: 47 Lansdowne

Psyche A boutique that handpicks the best Canadian and European clothing for men and women: great for cocktail as well as summer dresses. ⓐ 708 Queen St W ⓣ 416-599-4882 ⓛ 11.30–19.00 Mon–Wed, 11.30–20.00 Thur & Fri, 11.00–18.30 Sat, 12.00–18.00 Sun ⓝ Streetcar: 501 Queen, 511 Bathurst

Rotate This A perennial favourite for music in the city – this tiny store manages to cram in an awesome collection of the latest releases as well as vinyl classics. ⓐ 801 Queen St W ⓣ 416-504-8447 ⓦ www.rotate.com ⓛ 11.30–20.00 Mon–Fri, 10.30–20.00 Sat, 12.00–19.00 Sun ⓝ Streetcar: 501 Queen, 511 Bathurst

Soundscapes A veritable library of music, with some of the best in new indie and alternative releases. This is the place to find that artist you've searched for everywhere else. Also sells tickets to shows taking place in Toronto. ⓐ 572 College St ⓣ 416-537-1620 ⓦ www.soundscapesmusic.com ⓛ 10.00–23.00 Sun–Thur, 10.00–00.00 Fri & Sat ⓝ Streetcar: 506 Carlton, 511 Bathurst

Type Books Type is bucking the trend of struggling bookstores. Its largest location on Queen Street West has a cutesy yet elegant décor and is stocked with well-picked books anyone would splurge on. ⓐ 883 Queen St W ⓣ 416-366-8973 ⓦ www.typebooks.ca ⓛ 10.00–18.00 Mon–Wed, 10.00–19.00 Thur–Sat, 11.00–18.00 Sun ⓝ Streetcar: 501 Queen, 511 Bathurst

---

◗ *Toronto has plenty of choice when it comes to fashion*

TAKING A BREAK

Bacchus Roti Shop £ ❶ Come here for real deal Caribbean
food (succulent goat roti or spicy-sweet jerk chicken wings)
inside a little storefront in Parkdale. 🅰 1376 Queen St W
📞 416-532-8191 🕐 11.00–21.00 Tues–Sat 🚊 Streetcar: 501 Queen;
bus: 47 Lansdowne

Clafouti £ ❷ A quaint French bakery that bakes and sells
not only clafoutis (a type of delicious fruit and custard pie),
but also tarts, croissants, brioche and bread. 🅰 915 Queen St W
📞 416-603-1935 🕐 09.00–17.00 Mon, 08.00–18.00 Tues–Sat,
09.00–17.00 Sun 🚊 Streetcar: 501 Queen, 511 Bathurst,
505 Dundas

Ezra's Pound £ ❸ A quirky corner café on Dundas Street
West, serving good coffee and sophisticated café fare: where
possible organic, local and homemade. 🅰 913 Dundas St W
📞 647-346-8448 🌐 www.ezraspound.com 🕐 08.15–17.00
Tues–Sun 🚊 Streetcar: 505 Dundas, 511 Bathurst; bus:
63 Ossington

The Knit Café £ ❹ With one wall exclusively made of cubby
holes filled with yarn, you can guess what goes down here.
This knitters' rendezvous makes for a soothing place to
enjoy a cup of coffee. 🅰 1050 Queen St W 📞 416-533-5648
🌐 www.theknitcafetoronto.com 🕐 10.00–22.00 Tues, 10.00–21.00
Thur, 10.00–19.00 Fri–Mon 🚊 Streetcar: 501 Queen; bus:
63 Ossington

Tacos El Asador £ **❺** A cramped, hot, loud cantina, but nudge your way to the back and sample the Salvadorian specialty: the *pupusa*. ⓐ 690 Bloor St W ❶ 416-538-9747 ● 12.00–21.00 Mon–Sat, 14.00–21.00 Sun Ⓝ Subway: Christie, Bathurst

White Squirrel Coffee Shop £ **❻** Named after the famed white squirrels in Trinity Bellwoods Park, this café is known for its homemade treats and serves some of the best ice cream in the city. ⓐ 907 Queen St W ❶ 647-428-4478 Ⓦ http://whitesquirrelcoffee.com ● 07.30–17.00 Mon–Fri, 08.30–17.30 Sat & Sun, winter; until 21.00 in summer Ⓝ Streetcar: 501 Queen, 511 Bathurst

⬥ *Try Tacos El Asador for some of the best Latin American food in the city*

◆ *Graffiti galore at Sneaky Dee's*

AFTER DARK

RESTAURANTS

Golden Turtle £ ❼ Back in Ossington Avenue's seedier days, the Golden Turtle was cranking out the best and cheapest Vietnamese fare in the city. It still is. ⓐ 125 Ossington Ave ❶ 416-531-1601 🕐 11.00–22.00 Wed–Mon, 11.00–15.00 Tues Ⓝ Streetcar: 501 Queen; bus: 63 Ossington

Pizzeria Libretto £ ❽ It's hard to get a table at this place, so popular are its pizzas, which are cooked for 90 seconds in a 480°C (900°F) wood-fired oven. The result is a perfectly cooked crust and unforgettable meal. ⓐ 221 Ossington Ave ❶ 416-532-8000 Ⓦ www.pizzerialibretto.com 🕐 17.00–23.00 Mon–Fri, 16.00–23.00 Sat & Sun Ⓝ Streetcar: 505 Dundas; bus: 63 Ossington

Rhino Bar & Grill £–££ ❾ This place should win an award for Toronto's best patio – not to mention the great selection of local beers on tap and the pool tables at the back. ⓐ 1249 Queen St W ❶ 416-535-8089 Ⓦ www.therhino.ca 🕐 11.00–02.00 Mon–Fri, 10.00–02.00 Sat & Sun Ⓝ Streetcar: 501 Queen; bus: 47 Lansdowne

Sneaky Dee's ❿ £–££ With a late-night restaurant and bar on the first floor and a concert venue upstairs, it's easy to while away an entire night at this alternative, graffiti-covered haunt. ⓐ 431 College St ❶ 416-603-3090 Ⓦ www.sneaky-dees.com 🕐 11.00–03.00 Mon & Tues, 11.00–04.00 Wed & Thur, 11.00–04.30 Fri & Sat, 09.00–03.00 Sun Ⓝ Streetcar: 511 Bathurst, 506 Carlton

BARS & CLUBS

The Beaver A narrow bar with a cool-kid clientele; this spot hosts rampaging DJ dance parties at night and then serves brunch the next morning. 1192 Queen St W 416-537-2768 www.thebeavertoronto.com 11.00–02.00 Mon–Fri, 10.00–02.00 Sat & Sun Streetcar: 501 Queen; bus: 47 Lansdowne

Hugh's Room Popular with the 40-something crowd, this place is a perfect sit-down venue for jazz nights. 2261 Dundas St W 416-531-6604 www.hughsroom.com Shows: 20.30; hours vary Subway: Dundas West; streetcar: 501 Queen, 505 Dundas

The Local Unsurprisingly, this bar caters to locals thirsty for a pint, but it lives up to its name with a friendly vibe and good tunes. 396 Roncesvalles Ave 416-535-6225 http://thelocalpub.ca 15.00–03.00 Subway: Dundas West; streetcar: 505 Dundas, 501W Queen

Margret With a DJ spinning vinyl most nights, local fare and old-fashioned cocktails, this bar can keep you entertained all night. 2952 Dundas West 416-762-3373 20.00–02.00 Streetcar: 505 Dundas; bus: 41 Keele

Reposado A tequila bar which is single-handedly changing the oft-reviled drink's reputation with its spicy Bloody Caesars and sweet Margaritas. 136 Ossington Ave 416-532-6474 www.reposadobar.com 18.00–02.00 Mon–Thur, 14.00–02.00 Fri–Sun Streetcar: 501 Queen; bus: 63 Ossington

The Social A bit of a meat market for hipsters, but this club still puts on a reliably rambunctious dance party almost every night of the week. ⓐ 1100 Queen St W ⓣ 416-532-4474 ⓦ www.thesocial.ca ⓛ 22.00–late Mon–Sat; hours vary ⓝ Streetcar: 501 Queen; bus: 63 Ossington, 47 Lansdowne

Stone's Place Rolling Stones fans will love it here: walls are plastered in memorabilia and the plush couches and satin curtains give the place a nostalgic feel. ⓐ 1255 Queen St W ⓣ 416-536-4242 ⓦ www.stonesplace.ca ⓛ 21.00–02.00 Fri & Sat ⓝ Streetcar: 501 Queen; bus: 47 Lansdowne. Admission charge

Victory Café An unpretentious bar, popular with a younger crowd who prefer drinking and talking to dancing. Good beer selection and patio in the summer months. ⓐ 581 Markham St ⓣ 416-516-5787 ⓦ www.victorycafe.ca ⓛ 16.00–02.00 Mon–Fri, 14.00–02.00 Sat & Sun ⓝ Subway: Bathurst, Christie; bus: 94 Wellesley

Wrongbar One of Parkdale's only clubs with a wide range of themed nights: dance parties, concerts or punk-rock mosh pits. ⓐ 1279 Queen St W ⓣ 416-516-8677 ⓦ www.wrongbar.com ⓛ 22.00–late; hours vary ⓝ Streetcar: 501 Queen; bus: 47 Lansdowne

East End

Often neglected by visitors on short-break trips to Toronto, this part of the city is full of hidden gems and has the added bonus of being more relaxed and crowd-free than Downtown and the West End. The East End is mainly populated by young families, with strong Indian, Greek and Muslim communities.

Several areas deserve particular attention. Leslieville, which starts after Broadview Avenue along Queen Street East and runs to Leslie Street, has a great selection of brunch spots, coffee shops, restaurants and cocktail bars, but not too many late-night clubs. The Beaches, named for the long stretch of beach that borders the neighbourhood, is popular with families and dog-owners and manages to retain a relaxed, out-of-town feel even when packed with visitors in the summer. Greektown, stretching along Danforth Avenue at Broadview, is where eating, drinking and carousing go on until late into the night, while the Gerrard India Bazaar gets crowded in summer with barbecues and street vendors on every corner.

SIGHTS & ATTRACTIONS

The Don Jail
The city's notorious prison, in operation from 1864 to 1977, offers occasional tours through the well-preserved but gritty interiors. Up until Canada's last case of capital punishment took place here in 1962, 34 prisoners were executed in this jail alone. Ghost tours now make much of its supposedly haunted buildings. A kitschy and rather gruesome place to visit. ⓐ 550 Gerrard St E

🕿 416-470-6717 Ⓦ www.thedonjail.com 🕔 Tour times vary; call for details Ⓝ Subway: Broadview; streetcar: 506 Carlton, 504 King

East Chinatown

Not as overwhelming as the Downtown version but still worth a visit, Toronto's second Chinatown is a much more manageable option for scouting out dim sum eateries and Chinese bakeries. Ⓐ Gerrard St & Broadview Ave Ⓝ Subway: Broadview; streetcar: 506 Carlton, 504 King

🔺 *You know when you're in Leslieville*

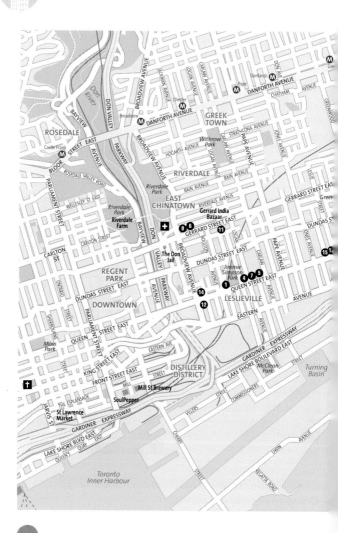

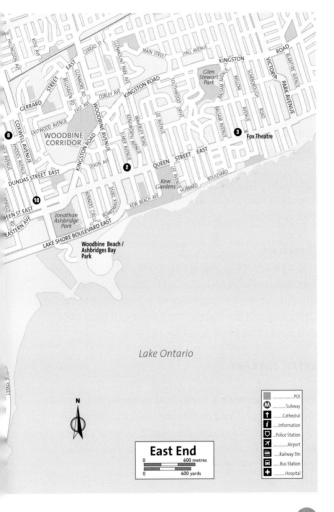

Gerrard India Bazaar

Every big city has its 'Little India', and Toronto's is the area known as the Gerrard India Bazaar, a quaint cluster of fabric and bangle stores, *paan* shops and tandoori houses in the city's vibrant East End. The bazaar is only a tiny remnant of the large Indian and Pakistani communities that used to live in this area but have now relocated to the suburbs outside Toronto. Still, it's a place to experience real Indian food and street life: in the warmer months, snack stalls are set up along the sidewalks offering everything from lime masala corn on the cob to crispy deep-fried *pakora* and dripping homemade *kulfi*. ⓐ Gerrard St E & Carlaw Ave Ⓝ Streetcar: 506 Carlton; bus: 22 Coxwell

Greektown

Home to one of the largest Greek communities in North America, Danforth Avenue's Greektown is in its own world of sambuca and flaming halloumi. A great place to dine and dance late into the night. ⓐ Danforth Ave at Broadview Ⓝ Subway: Broadview; streetcar: 504 King

RETAIL THERAPY

The Carrot Common A health food complex complete with juice bar, natural food market and medicine dispensary. ⓐ 348 Danforth Ave ⓣ 416-466-2644 Ⓦ www.carrotcommon.com ⓛ 09.00–21.00 Mon–Fri, 09.00–20.00 Sat, 11.00–18.00 Sun Ⓝ Subway: Pape, Chester

⬥ *Colourful trinkets for sale in Gerrard India Bazaar*

Doll Factory by Damzels Funky designer pieces are on display here, making it a good place to shop for accessories and unique gifts. 🅐 1122 Queen St E 🅣 416-598-0509 🅦 www.damzels.com 🅛 11.00–18.00 Tues–Sat, 12.00–17.00 Sun 🅝 Streetcar: 501 Queen; bus: 72 Pape

EyeSpy A cornucopia of gifts: from Hunter rubber boots and handmade notebooks to yo-yos and pinhole cameras. 🅐 388 Carlaw Ave, suite 200B 🅣 416-461-4061 🅦 www.eyespygifts.com 🅛 12.00–18.00 Mon–Sat, 12.00–17.00 Sun 🅝 Streetcar: 501 Queen; bus: 38 Jones

Winkel An anything-goes shop, where you can find quirky items to decorate the house: vintage posters, random button collections, handmade crafts and old wallpaper. 🅐 1107 Queen St E 🅣 416-465-4247 🅦 www.shopwinkel.blogspot.com 🅛 12.00–18.00 Wed–Sat, 12.00–17.00 Sun 🅝 Streetcar: 501 Queen; bus: 72 Pape

Zig Zag Vintage furniture at a good price: look for teak cabinets and wonky glass lamps. 🅐 985 Queen St E 🅣 416-778-6495 🅦 www.modfurnishings.com 🅛 12.00–17.30 Mon & Wed–Sat, 12.00–17.00 Sun 🅝 Streetcar: 501 Queen; bus: 72 Pape

TAKING A BREAK

Bonjour Brioche £ ❶ A French bakery that is tough to beat for brunch – expect to queue at weekends if you want to try its wonderful French toast and croissants. 🅐 812 Queen St E 🅣 416-406-1250 🅛 08.00–16.00 Tues–Sun 🅝 Streetcar: 501 Queen, 504 King

FOOD-IVERSITY

Almost nowhere is Toronto's multiculturalism more visible than in the mix of restaurants in the East End, with just about every nationality represented and fusion foods appearing on many menus.

For breakfast, choose between buttery croissants at Bonjour Brioche (see opposite) and, on a Sunday, a full-works Irish breakfast at The Roy Public House (see page 104); at lunchtime be tempted by dim sum at Pearl Court (see page 100), vegetable thali at Udupi Palace (see page 101) or real Italian pizza at Gio Rana's (see page 103). For dinner, there's refined Vietnamese cuisine on offer at the Hanoi 3 Seasons, German schnitzel at The Citizen, and classic French specialities at the Batifole bistro (see page 102), which is rather incongruously located in the middle of East Chinatown. Then go Russian for the evening at the Rasputin Vodka Bar (see page 104), or spend a night watching Spanish dancing at Embrujo Flamenco (see page 103).

Dufflet's Pastries £ ❷ A bona fide Toronto success story, this little bakery has made excellent treats since 1975 that are now hugely popular around town. If a café or restaurant doesn't make its own desserts, it's likely they come from Dufflets. The Queen Street East shop has a bright, playful feel and serves all the favourites.
ⓐ 1917 Queen St E ❶ 416-699-4900 ⓦ www.dufflet.com
🕐 09.00–19.00 Mon–Thur, 09.00–22.00 Fri, 10.00–22.00 Sat, 11.00–18.00 Sun ⓝ Streetcar: 501 Queen; bus: 64 Main, 91 Woodbine

Ed's Real Scoop £ ❸ Ed dominates the East End for homemade ice cream, with a great location at The Beaches. **ⓐ** 2224 Queen St E **ⓣ** 416-699-6100 **ⓛ** 11.00–21.30 **ⓝ** Streetcar: 501 Queen; bus: 64 Main

Lady Marmalade £ ❹ A bright, colourful spot that's only recently arrived in the Leslieville 'hood but is already popular for its all-day breakfast menu. **ⓐ** 898 Queen St E **ⓣ** 647-351-7645 **ⓦ** www.ladymarmalade.ca **ⓛ** 08.00–16.00 Mon–Sat **ⓝ** Streetcar: 501 Queen; bus: 72 Pape

Mercury Espresso Bar £ ❺ This place takes its coffee seriously with an espresso so deliciously bitter it makes your lips pucker with pleasure. **ⓐ** 915 Queen St E **ⓣ** 647-435-4779 **ⓦ** mercuryorganic.blogspot.com **ⓛ** 06.30–21.00 Mon–Fri, 07.00–21.00 Sat & Sun **ⓝ** Streetcar: 501 Queen; bus: 72 Pape

Pearl Court £ ❻ A sprawling dim sum palace, filled with plastic sheeted tables and clattering carts dispensing deep-fried goodness. The Pearl Court regularly tops 'best in the city' lists for dim sum. **ⓐ** 633 Gerrard St E **ⓣ** 416-463-8778 **ⓛ** 08.00–15.00 Sun–Tue, Thur, 08.00–16.00 Wed, Fri & Sat **ⓝ** Subway: Broadview; streetcar: 506 Gerrard, 504 King, 505 Dundas

Leslieville Cheese Market £–££ ❼ A cheese shop that doubles as a take-away. A local favourite is the grilled cheese and pineapple sandwich. **ⓐ** 891 Queen St E **ⓣ** 416 465-7143 **ⓦ** www.leslievillecheese.com **ⓛ** 10.00–19.00 Mon–Fri,

09.30–19.00 Sat, 11.00–18.00 Sun ⊙ Streetcar: 501 Queen; bus: 72 Pape ❶ Closes 1 hr earlier Sat & Sun, Jan & Feb

Udupi Palace £–££ ❻ Don't come to this cafeteria-style restaurant in a tiled underground basement for the atmosphere, but you mustn't miss its vegetarian thali served with raita or its other excellent curries. ❸ 1460 Gerrard St E ❶ 416-405-8189 ⓦ www.udupipalace.ca ❺ 12.00–22.00 Sun–Thur, 12.00–23.00 Fri & Sat ⊙ Streetcar: 506 Carlton; bus: 22 Coxwell

🔺 Savour the excellent Indian food at Udupi Palace

AFTER DARK

RESTAURANTS

Hanoi 3 Seasons £ ❾ Set apart from the other slightly dodgy eateries that surround it, Hanoi has a refined dining space and delicious Vietnamese fare. Try the breaded grouper. ⓐ 588 Gerrard St E ① 416-463-9940 ⓛ 12.00–15.00, 18.00–23.00 Tues–Sun Ⓝ Subway: Broadview; streetcar: 506 Gerrard, 504 King, 505 Dundas

The Tulip £ ❿ The East End's best steakhouse has been around since the 1920s, serving the cheapest, most succulent steak imaginable. The cardiac-arrest inducing breakfast, Steak 'n' Eggs, is the perfect hangover remedy according to some. ⓐ 1610 Queen St E ① 416-469-5797 Ⓦ www.tulipsteakhouse.com ⓛ 08.00–23.00 Ⓝ Streetcar: 501 Queen; bus: 22 Coxwell

Batifole ££ ⓫ This classic French bistro smack bang in the middle of East Chinatown draws foodies from across the city with its laid-back atmosphere and unpretentious nosh. ⓐ 744 Gerrard St E ① 416-462-9965 Ⓦ www.batifole.ca ⓛ 18.00–22.30 Wed–Mon Ⓝ Subway: Broadview; streetcar: 506 Carlton, 504 King

The Citizen ££ ⓬ Serving German dishes such as spaetzel and schnitzel with an interesting twist. The Caesar salad with poached egg is beloved amongst locals in Leslieville, as is the wide beer selection. ⓐ 730 Queen St E ① 416-465-0100 Ⓦ www.therosebud.ca ⓛ 17.00–22.00 Mon–Wed, 17.00–23.00 Thur–Sat Ⓝ Streetcar: 501 Queen, 504 King

Gio Rana's Really Really Nice Restaurant ££ ⑬ You won't see the name printed on this quirky restaurant, but look out for a big nose over the top the door marking the spot. Come for modern Italian food, done really, really nice. ⓐ 1220 Queen St E ⓣ 416-469-5225 ⓛ 18.00–23.00 Tues–Thur, 18.00–00.00 Fri & Sat, 18.00–22.30 Sun ⓝ Streetcar: 501 Queen; bus: 31 Greenwood

Pic Nic ££ ⑭ Toronto loves communal tables and charcuterie, and this Leslieville spot delivers on this trend with shared platters of meats and cheeses paired with local wines. ⓐ 747 Queen St E ⓣ 647-435-5298 ⓦ www.picnicwinebar.com ⓛ 17.00–20.00 Mon–Fri, 17.00–00.00 Sat ⓝ Streetcar: 501 Queen, 504 King

Tomi Kro ££ ⑮ A Leslieville favourite that serves excellent mojitos and an inventive fusion of North American, Mediterranean and Asian cooking inside its three meandering dining rooms. ⓐ 1214 Queen St E ⓣ 416-463-6677 ⓛ 18.00–22.00 Mon–Wed, 18.00–23.00 Thur–Sat ⓝ Streetcar: 501 Queen; bus: 31 Greenwood, 72 Pape

BARS & CLUBS

The Curzon A new addition to the Queen Street East stretch, the after-dinner crowd from Tomi Kro, Gio Rana and Leslie Jones spill in here for party snacks and cocktails later in the evening. ⓐ 1192 Queen St E ⓣ 416-850-3650 ⓛ 17.00–02.00 ⓝ Streetcar: 501 Queen; bus: 72 Pape

Embrujo Flamenco An authentic Spanish tavern serving delicious tapas accompanied by a live flamenco show on certain evenings during the week. At weekends, dinner seatings are organised around three live shows at 18.00, 20.00 and 22.00. ⓐ 97 Danforth Ave ⓣ 416-778-0007 ⓦ www.embrujoflamenco.com ⓛ 18.00–23.00 Mon–Wed, 17.00–23.00 Thur–Sun; brunch: 11.00–14.00 Sat & Sun ⓝ Streetcar: 501 Queen, 504 King

The Opera House One of the East End's few live music venues, The Opera House started out in the early 1900s as a vaudeville venue and now puts on heavy metal shows and other hardcore acts. Not for fans of Puccini. ⓐ 735 Queen St E ⓣ 416-466-0313 ⓦ www.theoperahousetoronto.com ⓛ Times vary depending on event ⓝ Streetcar: 501 Queen, 504 King

Rasputin Vodka Bar Candles, gaudy chandeliers and row upon row of vodka bottles fill the innards of this cavernous Russian drinking hole. DJs spin house beats on Wednesdays to Saturdays. ⓐ 780 Queen St E ⓣ 416-469-3737 ⓦ www.rasputinvodkabar.com ⓛ 17.00–00.00 Tues & Wed, 17.00–02.00 Thur & Fri, 19.00–02.00 Sat ⓝ Streetcar: 501 Queen, 504 King

The Roy Public House One of the few true British pubs in the area, The Roy has a good selection of beer and British staples: think shepherd's pie, fish and chips… The full Irish breakfast is a treat after a late Saturday night. ⓐ 894 Queen St E ⓣ 416-465-3331 ⓦ www.theroy.ca ⓛ 11.00–02.00 Thur–Sat, 11.00–01.00 Sun–Wed ⓝ Streetcar: 501 Queen

▶ *Rows of young grapevines growing in a Niagara vineyard*

OUT OF TOWN
trips

The Niagara region

The towering horseshoe-shaped Niagara Falls are a world-famous attraction, but they are not all this fascinating region has to offer. Niagara-on-the-Lake, a small town on the US border, figured prominently in the War of 1812 between Canada and the US and has preserved many of its original buildings from that time. Visitors flock here for its serene feel, beautiful gardens, 19th-century houses and rich history. Other attractions are scattered nearby, including the Laura Secord homestead and several world-class wineries.

Niagara Falls, a short drive away, is on the banks of the iconic waterfalls that have been a tourist destination for over 150 years. The downtown area is touristy, with haunted houses, wax museums and mini golf courses. In terms of accommodation and dining, you're better off at Niagara-on-the-Lake.

Note that both Niagara-on-the-Lake and Niagara Falls are tourist hotspots that gear up from late spring (around 22 May) until late autumn. Out of season, many attractions have sporadic hours or are closed altogether.

Gateway Niagara Information Centre ⓐ 424 South Service Rd, Grimsby (along Highway 405, just past Hamilton) ⓘ 905-945-5444 ⓦ www.tourismniagara.com ⓒ 08.30–19.00 July & Aug, 09.00–18.00 Sept–June

Niagara-on-the-Lake Visitor & Convention Bureau ⓐ 26 Queen St ⓘ 905-468-1950 ⓦ www.niagaraonthelake.com ⓒ 10.00–19.30 May–Oct; 10.00–17.00 Nov–Apr

Niagara Falls Tourism ⓐ 5535 Stanley Ave, off Murray St ⓘ 905-356-6061 ⓦ www.niagarafallstourism.com

⬥ *The great curve and surge of the Canadian Niagara Falls*

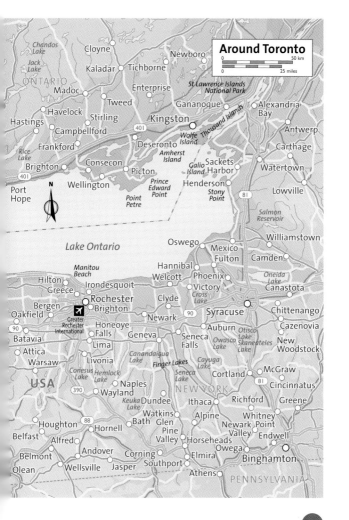

Around Toronto

0 — 50 km
0 — 25 miles

GETTING THERE

The Niagara region lies around 120 km (75 miles) south of
Toronto. VIA Rail Canada (see page 128) runs two to three trains
per day to Niagara Falls or the nearby town of St. Catharines.
GO Transit (see page 129) offers five rail services a day to Niagara
Falls and St. Catharines on weekends and holidays in summer.
Greyhound and Coach Canada buses (see page 129) have seven
or eight daily departures from Toronto to Niagara Falls and St.
Catharines. Shuttles run from St. Catharines to Niagara-on-the-
Lake and Niagara Falls, but you must pre-book this service by phone
(☎ 905-468-1950) or online at ⓦ www.niagaraonthelake.com.

CYCLING AROUND NIAGARA

In the warmer months, keen cyclists can pop
their bikes on the **Niagara Greenbelt Express train**
(ⓦ www.niagaragreenbelt.com) that runs seasonally from
Toronto's Union Station to Niagara Falls Station. On arrival,
spin over to the nearby Falls, then cycle north along the
Niagara River Recreation trail that runs for 20 km (12 miles)
past the Niagara Gorge, via many wineries and right into
Niagara-on-the-Lake. Or ride the path south for 35 km
(22 miles), where you'll find, along with a beautiful white
sand beach, the historic **Fort Erie** (⊕ 350 Lakeshore Rd,
Fort Erie ☎ 905-871-0540 ⓦ www.1812-bicentennial.ca
🕙 10.00–17.00 early May–early Oct. Admission charge),
scene of one of the bloodiest battles in Canadian history.

A regular bus, **5-0 Taxi** (☏ 905-358-3232 ⓦ www.5-otaxi.com), links
Niagara-on-the-Lake with the Niagara Falls during high season.

To reach the Niagara region by car takes around two hours.
Take Highway 403, then Highway 407, which becomes 405. After
St. Catharines, either take Highway 55 to Niagara-on-the-Lake,
or continue on until Highway 420, which goes into Niagara Falls.

NIAGARA FALLS

SIGHTS & ATTRACTIONS
Niagara Falls
The name 'Niagara Falls' actually refers to two waterfalls,
American and Canadian respectively, which sit side by side
along the Niagara River. At just 57.3 m (188 ft) in height but an
incredible 670 m (2,200 ft) in width, the Canadian Falls dwarf
their American counterpart. The rounded horseshoe shape of
the Canadian Falls creates a plume of mist which, accompanied
by the thundering sound of 168,000 cubic metres (6 million
cubic feet) of water flowing over the edge every minute, makes
the Falls a wondrous sight.

The water coursing through this area is left over from the
last Ice Age, at the end of which, around 12,500 years ago, the
Niagara Peninsula became free of ice and the melting water
flowed into Lake Erie, Lake Ontario and the Niagara River. 5,000
years ago, the waters of the Niagara River scourged open an older
riverbed, creating a sharp drop in the river and continuing to
erode the edge, which recesses at the rate of around a foot per
year. Currently, the water provided by the Falls serves more than
a million people in both the US and Canada for drinking water,

hydropower and fishing, along with a variety of other purposes.

There's an observation deck at the base of the Falls, where you can get a front-row seat to the thundering deluge. However, to experience the downpour in all its glory, it's a good idea to take one of the other viewing options on offer – those listed below and opposite. For more information about the Falls, see ⓦ www.niagaraparks.com.

Journey Behind the Falls

An interactive experience of the Falls, with an elevator that descends 46 m (150 ft) through bedrock to tunnels that give a glimpse of the water from behind. The tour, which lasts 30–45 minutes, also features a visit to the Falls' observation deck, where the ponchos they provide are certainly needed. ⓐ 6650 Niagara Parkway, behind Table Rock Centre ⓛ 09.00–22.00 summer; 09.00–18.00 Mon–Fri, 09.00–21.00 Sat & Sun, winter. Admission charge

Maid of the Mist

This traditional ferry ride has taken visitors floating past the falls since 1846. The boat comes right up to the edge of the deluge, making for an exhilarating (and wet) half-hour ride. ⓐ 5920 Niagara Parkway ⓣ 905-358-5781 ⓦ www.maidofthemist.com ⓛ 09.00–19.00 mid-Apr–Aug; 09.45–16.45 Sept–mid-Oct. Admission charge ❶ Dependent upon weather conditions

Niagara's Fury

The most bombastic experience of the Falls, featuring a six-minute version of how the drop was created, complete with shaking floor,

DON'T TRY THIS AT HOME
A 63-year old schoolteacher, Annie Taylor, was the first to go over the Falls and survive. She accomplished the stunt in a barrel, along with her cat, in 1901.

a 20°C temperature drop and spraying water. ⓐ 6650 Niagara Parkway ⓦ www.niagarasfury.com ⓛ 10.00–17.00. Admission charge

White Water Walk
A boardwalk at the foot of Niagara's tremendous Great Gorge is reached by an elevator that descends to the Whirlpool Rapids, a short distance from the Falls themselves. ⓐ 4330 Niagara Parkway ⓣ 905-371-0254 ⓛ 10.00–17.00 Mar–9 May; 10.00–18.00 Mon–Fri, 09.00–19.00 Sat & Sun, 9 May–27 June; 09.00–20.00 27 June–6 Sept; 10.00–17.00 Mon–Fri, 10.00–18.00 Sat & Sun 7 Sept–mid-Oct. Admission charge ⓘ Dependent upon weather conditions

NIAGARA-ON-THE-LAKE

SIGHTS & ATTRACTIONS
Fort George
American forces destroyed this fort during the War of 1812 between the US and Canada. The fort has since been rebuilt to its original state and houses a museum. ⓐ Off Niagara Parkway, south of Niagara-on-the-Lake ⓣ 905-468-0888 ⓦ www.friendsoffortgeorge.ca ⓛ 10.00–17.00 summer; 10.00–17.00 Sat & Sun, winter. Admission charge

Laura Secord Homestead

Laura Secord may be better known, these days, for the chocolate and ice cream company named after her, but she is actually a national hero from the War of 1812. The home she lived in more than 200 years ago, in the small town of Queenston between Niagara Falls and Niagara-on-the-Lake, has been restored to that time period. ⓐ 29 Queenston St, Queenston ⓦ www.niagaraparks.com ⓛ 09.30–15.30 Mon–Fri, 11.00–17.00 Sat & Sun, May–June; 11.00–17.00 July–Aug; 11.00–17.00 Wed–Sun Sept–early Oct. Admission charge

CULTURE

Niagara Historical Society Museum

This museum is a treasure trove of history and artworks relating to Niagara-on-the-Lake and its surrounding area. ⓐ 43 Castlereagh St

▲ The picturesque main street in Niagara-on-the-Lake

WINE TOUR

With a car, a map and a couple of sunny days, you can take one of the best wine tours that Canada has to offer. The Niagara region's wineries generally offer tours and tastings as well as wine fairs, occasional concerts, and special meals, and some have restaurants. The pick of the bunch are listed below, but there are plenty of others, including the up-and-coming **Peller Estates Winery** (ⓐ 290 John St E ⓣ 905-468-4678 ⓦ www.peller.com ⓛ 10.00–21.00 summer; 10.00–18.00 winter) for its award-winning ice wines and **Stratus Vineyards** (ⓐ 2059 Niagara Stone Rd ⓣ 905-468-1806 ⓦ www.stratuswines.com ⓛ 11.00–17.00), known for its eco-friendly practices.

Creekside Estate Winery One of the most popular wineries in the region, famed for its white wines and lovely weekend lunches. ⓐ 2170 Fourth Ave, Jordan ⓣ 905-562-0035 ⓦ www.creeksidewine.com ⓛ Winery: 10.00–17.00; tours: 14.00, May–Sept; restaurant: 12.00–16.00 Sat & Sun, May–Oct

Inniskillin The granddaddy of wineries in the region; it received the first wine-making licence since prohibition in the 1970s. ⓐ 1499 Line 3, off Niagara Parkway ⓣ 905-468-3554 ⓦ www.inniskillin.com ⓛ 09.00–18.00 summer; 09.00–17.00 winter

Jackson-Triggs A state-of-the-art facility designed by

Toronto firm KPMB. As the first to use a special eco-friendly 'gravity flow' process, Jackson-Triggs has established a trend in winemaking in the region. ⓐ 2145 Regional Road 55 ❶ 905-468-4637 Ⓦ www.jacksontriggswinery.com ❶ 10.30–17.00

❶ 905-468-3912 Ⓦ www.niagarahistorical.museum ❶ 10.00–17.00 summer; 13.00–17.00 winter. Admission charge

Shaw Festival

Niagara-on-the-Lake's theatres band together between April and October to host the Shaw Festival, whose patron playwright is George Bernard Shaw. Venues in Niagara-on-the-Lake include the vintage **Festival Theatre** (ⓐ 10 Queen's Parade), the Edwardian-style **Royal George Theatre** (ⓐ 85 Queen St) and the **Court House Theatre** (ⓐ 26 Queen St), where the Shaw Festival first began. For further information, contact the festival office at ❶ 905-468-2153 or Ⓦ www.shawfest.com.

TAKING A BREAK & AFTER DARK

McFarland House £ Built in the 1800s by one of the area's first settlers, with tea, wine and treats served in a period garden. ⓐ 15927 Niagara Parkway ❶ 905-468-3322 ❶ 12.00–17.00 ❶ Closed in winter

Victoria Gallery £ A historic spot which serves over 150 different types of teas and a good selection of coffees. Built in 1812, it's the longest established commercial building in Upper Canada (an older name for southern Ontario). ⓐ 108 Queen St ⓣ 905-468-0381 ⓦ www.victoriateas.com ⓛ 10.00–18.00 Mon–Thur, 10.00–19.00 Fri, 10.00–20.00 Sat & Sun

The Olde Angel Inn ££ Lively in the evening, this 200-year old inn survived the War of 1812 and now serves classic British fare on the first floor. Also offers rooms for rent. ⓐ 224 Regent St ⓣ 905-468-3411 ⓦ www.angel-inn.com ⓛ 11.00–01.00

Charles Inn £££ A candle-lit restaurant inside a Georgian-style mansion, with a six-course tasting menus of foie gras and duck magret. ⓐ 209 Queen St ⓣ 905-468-4588 ⓦ www.charlesinn.ca ⓛ 17.00–22.30

ACCOMMODATION

Many private homes in Niagara-on-the-Lake offer B&B accommodation, with rates from $100–300 a night. See ⓦ www.niagaraonthelake.com for a selection.

Queen's Landing ££ With its wallpapered rooms and wooden beds, this spot has a quaint feeling but still features the amenities of a large-scale hotel with its whirl and salt-water pools and a grand dining room. ⓐ 155 Byron St ⓣ 905-468-2195 ⓦ www.vintage-hotels.com

The Prince of Wales £££ A beautifully preserved Victorian-style hotel which serves a traditional high tea every afternoon. ⓐ 6 Picton St ⓣ 905-468-3246 ⓦ www.vintage-hotels.com

Stratford

Just 150 km (93 miles) southwest of Toronto, Stratford makes for a pleasant cultural day trip from the city. The downtown core is a perfectly preserved 19th-century small Canadian town, with its red brick houses, gorgeous parks and turn-of-the-century palatial estates. The city's history spans over 175 years and, despite its name, Stratford didn't always seem destined to become the theatrical hub it is now. Until the 1960s, trains, shipping and the furniture industry fuelled Stratford's economy. In the early 1900s, the sprawling Upper Queens Park was established, laying the groundwork for the parks that are now the city's trademark.

Simply walking around Stratford's quaint streets admiring historic buildings such as the City Hall (see page 120) and the **St James Anglican Church** (📍 6 Hamilton St ☎ 519-271-3572 🕐 10.00–13.30) is a treat in itself; the tourist board offers guided walks and themed culinary tours in summer. Or head further out to the Avon River, along whose banks are meandering paths and picnic spots, with weeping willows and bridges draping over the water. **Avon Boat Rentals** (📍 40 York St ☎ 519-271-7739 🕐 10.00–19.00) rents out paddle boats, canoes and kayaks to explore the lagoons hidden along the river, where the swans of Stratford are usually seen. These birds are famous in the city and have their own parade – the Annual Swan Release on the first Sunday of April. During the parade, as many as two dozen swans (along with other waterfowl) march down the city streets from their winter home to the Avon River, escorted by a marching band and bagpiper.

As well as the famous Stratford Shakespeare Festival, it's

St James Anglican Church

worth timing your visit to coincide with the **Stratford Summer Music Festival** (ⓦ www.stratfordsummermusic.ca), which takes place here from mid-July to mid-August and draws classical ensembles, orchestras and choirs from around the world as well as jazz singers, cabaret and blues acts.

Stratford Tourism Alliance ⓐ 47 Downie St ⓣ 519-271-5140
ⓦ www.welcometostratford.com ⓛ 08.30–16.30 Mon–Fri, Jan–end May; 08.30–17.00 Mon–Fri, end May–Sept; 08.30–16.30 Mon–Fri, 10.00–18.00 Sat & Sun, Oct; 08.30–16.30 Mon–Fri, 10.00–14.00 Sat, Nov & Dec

York Street Visitor Kiosk ⓐ York St Parking Lot, Lakeside Drive
ⓣ 1-800-561-7926 ⓛ 10.00–18.00 June–Sept

GETTING THERE

Stratford is easily reached by car, train or bus. Three trains leave Toronto Union Station for Stratford on weekdays (two on Saturday), taking around two hours and 20 minutes. Greyhound buses (see page 129) are slightly cheaper and leave more frequently with over ten departures every day, but the trip takes nearly three hours as you must transfer at Kitchener. By car, take Highway 401 to Kitchener, then Highway 8 west to Stratford.

SIGHTS & ATTRACTIONS

City Hall
Built at the turn of the 19th century when a fire destroyed its predecessor, the attractive red brick geometric building is built in the Queen Anne Revival style and is a hallmark of Stratford.

COUNTRY LIFE

Those interested in back-to-basics living might be interested to see the horses and buggies of Stratford's traditionally secretive Amish Mennonite community, who live an electricity- and car-free existence. The community is just starting to open up, offering tours that give a sneak peek into this pre-industrial lifestyle and allow visitors to purchase Amish leather goods and crafts. Contact the tourist office for more information.

No tours are offered, but you're free to wander in and admire the Council Chambers. ⓐ 1 Wellington St ⓣ 519-271-0250 ⓦ www.city.stratford.on.ca ⓛ 08.30–16.30 Mon–Fri

Parks & gardens

Stratford is an incredibly green city, with many lush and pristine parks. All of its gardens are free of charge and open 24 hours a day. The **Arthur Meighen Gardens** (ⓐ 55 Queen St ⓣ 519-273-1600 ⓛ Tours: 11.00 Wed–Sat, June–Sept) in front of the Festival Theatre are perfect for strolling around in before a show and offer tours for a small fee. The **Millennium Park** (ⓐ 54 Romeo St ⓣ 519-271-0250) just outside the Gallery Stratford, is another community favourite with its beautiful fountain and sculptures, while the **Shakespearean Gardens** (ⓐ Huron St Bridge) are styled after the carefully-preened English Garden. For a more intense hike, try the **Avon Trail** (ⓦ www.avontrail.ca) that stretches 104 km (65 miles) through scenic farmland.

⬢ *Summer house in the pretty Shakespearean Gardens*

STRATFORD SHAKESPEARE FESTIVAL

Stratford attracts thespians from around the world to its famous annual theatre festival, which gears up every April and runs until early November. Everything from Shakespeare to modern works are on show, with the programme changing every year. Tickets are sold at the central **Festival Theatre** (@ 55 Queen St @ 1-800-567-1600 @ www.stratfordfestival.ca @ 09.00–20.00 Mon–Sat, 09.00–14.00 Sun, Apr–Nov), and run from $30 to over $100 depending on the show and venue. The Festival Theatre hosts the large-scale productions: its trap doors and multiple levels make it ideal for a staging of *A Midsummer's Night Dream* or *The Tempest*. To see the inner workings of the theatre as well as the prop and wardrobe department, go on a **backstage tour** (@ 09.00, 09.15 Wed–Sat, June–Oct). There's also a **costume warehouse tour** (@ 350 Douro St @ 10.00, 10.30, 11.00, 11.30 Wed–Sat, May–Oct). As well as the Festival Theatre, plays are staged at the **Avon Theatre** (@ 99 Downie St), **Tom Patterson Theatre** (@ 111 Lakeside Drive) and **Studio Theatre** (@ 34 George St E).

Stratford Farmers' Market

The twice-weekly market is a great introduction to small-town Canadian life. Local farmers sell fruit, vegetables, summer sausage (a type of sausage that doesn't need refrigeration) and crafts, while the close-knit Amish community (see page 121) also turns up to sell handmade lip balm, candles and other products.

@ 353 McCarthy Rd ① 519-271-5130 ⓦ www.stratfordfairgrounds.com
① 15.00–19.00 Wed, 07.00–12.00 Sat

CULTURE

Factory 163

What once housed the Globe Wernike Company, which built
furniture in the city's one-time booming industry, has become
a hub for arts and culture. @ 163 King St ① 519-275-2391
ⓦ www.factory163.com ① Times vary

Gallery Stratford

Stratford's largest art gallery displays the work of local, national
and international visual artists. The permanent collection has over
1,000 pieces of art, mainly from Canadian artists. @ 54 Romeo St S
① 519-271-5271 ⓦ www.gallerystratford.on.ca ① 10.00–17.00 Tues–
Sun, summer; 12.00–16.00 Tues–Sun, winter. Admission charge

RETAIL THERAPY

Chocolate Barr's Candies Derek Barr, who worked for five years
at Rheo Thompson Candies, has now got his own shop selling
delicious cashew brittle and sponge toffee. @ 136 Ontario St
① 519-272-2828 ⓦ www.chocolatebarrs.com ① 09.00–18.00
Mon–Thur & Sat, 09.00–20.00 Fri

Family & Company A children's store that's fun for adults
too, with its distinctly Mr. Magorium's Wonder Emporium feel.
@ 6 Ontario St ① 519-273-7060 ⓦ www.familyandcompany.com

STRATFORD

🕐 09.30–19.45 Mon–Sat, 10.00–17.45 Sun, summer; 09.30–19.45 Mon–Fri, 09.30–17.45 Sat, 11.00–16.45 Sun, winter

Rheo Thompson Candies The granddaddy of chocolatiers in a city with a sweet tooth. Rheo Thompson has been in business since the late 1960s, making its trademark mint smoothie chocolates. ⓐ 55 Albert St ☎ 519-271-6910 ⓦ www.rheothompson.com 🕐 09.00–17.30 Mon–Sat, 11.00–15.00 Sun, May–Dec

TAKING A BREAK & AFTER DARK

Bentley's Restaurant £ Patrons cram this café-bar's wooden booths to spend the day lingering over a pint or coffee. It's a good place to grab some pub fare in the evening as well, and rooms are available for rent upstairs. ⓐ 99 Ontario St ☎ 519-271-1121 ⓦ www.bentleys-annex.com 🕐 11.00–02.00

The Church Restaurant ££ The exquisite French cuisine served inside a converted church makes for a wonderfully romantic meal. ⓐ 70 Brunswick St ☎ 519-273-3424 ⓦ www.churchrestaurant.com 🕐 17.00–20.30 Tues–Sat, 17.00–20.00 Sun

Old Prune Restaurant ££ The curmudgeonly name does not do this place justice, with its yummy fare and graceful, glassed-in garden dining room. ⓐ 151 Albert St ☎ 519-271-5052 ⓦ www.oldprune.on.ca 🕐 17.00–20.00 Tues–Sat 17.00–19.00 Sun ❶ Closed in winter

Rundles Restaurant ££ One of the most sophisticated spots to dine in Stratford, this restaurant has a modern cottage feel and

gastronomic cuisine. For a cheaper meal, head to the Rundles
Sophisto-Bistro inside, where nosh goes for almost half the price.
Pre-theatre menus available. ⓐ 9 Cobourg St ⓣ 519-271-6442
ⓦ www.rundlesrestaurant.com ⓛ 17.00–19.30 Tues & Sun,
17.00–20.30 Wed–Sat

ACCOMMODATION

Accommodation gets booked out quickly during the Stratford
Shakespeare Festival (see page 123). If you're in a fix, the Festival
Theatre information line may be able to suggest a local B&B
with available rooms.

SGH Residence £ For cheap digs, try the clean and well-kept dorm
and single rooms at SGH. An outdoor pool makes it a friendly
place to meet fellow travellers. ⓐ 130 Youngs St ⓣ 519-271-5084
ⓦ www.sgh.stratford.on.ca

Foster's Inn ££ A cosy place to bed down, located inside an early
19th-century heritage building downtown, with spa services,
a bar and restaurant on site. ⓐ 111 Downie St ⓣ 519-271-1119
ⓦ www.fostersinn.com

Mercer Hall Inn ££–£££ Situated on Stratford's main drag, only
steps away from the theatres. Rates include breakfast at the
Tango Café & Grill below. ⓐ 108 Ontario St ⓣ 519-271-1888
ⓦ www.mercerhallinn.com

◗ *Streetcar in Downtown Toronto*

PRACTICAL
information

Directory

GETTING THERE

By air

Most major airlines have direct flights to Toronto Pearson International Airport (see page 48). **British Airways** (ⓦ www.britishairways.com) and **Air Canada** (ⓦ www.aircanada.ca) fly direct from London Heathrow, while **Continental Airlines** (ⓦ www.continental.com), **United Airlines** (ⓦ www.united.com) and **Delta Airlines** (ⓦ www.delta.com) all offer flights from both UK and US cities. The Canadian national airline **Air Canada** (ⓦ www.aircanada.ca) runs direct flights from many major American cities to Toronto. **Qantas** (ⓦ www.qantas.com.au) flies from Sydney, Australia to Toronto, while **Air New Zealand** (ⓦ www.airnewzealand.com) fly from Auckland. **Porter Airlines** (ⓦ www.flyporter.com) fly to the Toronto City Centre Airport (see page 49) from other Canadian and North American cities.

Many people are aware that air travel emits CO_2, which contributes to climate change. You may be interested in the possibility of lessening the environmental impact of your flight through **Climate Care** (ⓦ www.climatecare.org), which offsets your CO_2 by funding environmental projects around the world.

By rail

VIA Rail Canada (ⓣ 1-888-842-7245 ⓦ www.viarail.ca) serves the whole country, arriving at and departing from Toronto's central Union Station (see page 52). The journey from Montreal to Toronto takes around five and a half hours, while a trip from Ottawa will take approximately four and a half hours. **Amtrak**

(☎ 1-800-872-7245 ⓦ www.amtrak.com) trains also leave from Union Station, running to American cities including Chicago and New York with several stopping points along the way. **GO Transit** (☎ 416-869-3200 ⓦ www.gotransit.com) trains link Toronto to all the nearby suburbs and larger cities including Hamilton, Guelph and Niagara Falls (see page 111).

By road
Greyhound (☎ 416-594-1010 ⓦ www.greyhound.ca), **Coach Canada** (☎ 1-800-461-7661 ⓦ www.coachcanada.com) and **Ontario Northland** (☎ 705-472-4500 ⓦ www.ontc.on.ca) coaches all arrive at and depart from Toronto Coach Terminal (see page 52), routing from many North American and Canadian cities. Driving

🔺 *Modern hall in Toronto Pearson International Airport*

to Toronto is a possibility, although note that journey times are long. If you arrive at a major US-Canada border during peak hours, expect to wait for up to an hour to cross. This is especially true at the Detroit-Windsor, Buffalo-Fort Erie and Niagara Falls-New York crossings.

ENTRY FORMALITIES

Citizens of the US, Australia, New Zealand and most EU countries do not need a visa in order to enter Canada and can remain for up to three months. South African citizens do require a visa, along with residents of the Czech Republic, Romania and, at the time of writing, Mexico. Polish and Lithuanian visitors who posses non-biometric passports should also acquire a visa before travelling to Canada. For more information on visa and immigration requirements, check the website of the **Department of Citizenship and Immigration** (Ⓦ www.cic.gc.ca).

Visitors over 19 can bring in alcohol up to the limits of one of the following variations: 1.5 litres of wine; 1.14 litres of liquor; or 24 x 355 millilitre containers of beer or ale. The duty-free tobacco allowance includes 200 cigarettes, 50 cigars or cigarillos, 200 grams of tobacco and 200 tobacco sticks. Carrying more than CAD$10,000 into the county needs to be reported at customs.

MONEY

Canada uses the Canadian dollar (CAD$), which consists of 100 cents (¢). Paper bills (notes) come in denominations of $5, $10, $20, $50 and $100. A $2 coin is referred to as a 'toonie', while $1 coins are called 'loonies'. You'll also see coins of 25¢ (a quarter),

10¢ (a dime), 5¢ (a nickel) and 1¢ (a penny). Note that Canadian dollars do not have the same value as US dollars; see Ⓦ www.xe.com to find out the latest exchange rates.

Most restaurants, stores and even taxis will accept major credit cards, including American Express, MasterCard and Visa, as well as debit cards. Smaller restaurants, cafés and shops sometimes accept only cash. ATMs are abundant in the Downtown tourist areas and are the easiest way to obtain Canadian dollars.

Ontario has a high tax rate, with a combined provincial and federal sales tax of 15 per cent on all purchases. The only stores in which tax is included in the listed price are liquor stores – everywhere else, including in restaurants and bars, prices are usually given without tax. Groceries, vitamins, medicine, feminine hygiene products and prepared food under $4 are not taxed.

HEALTH, SAFETY & CRIME

Toronto is generally a safe city to visit. Its restaurants and bars have a stringent hygiene inspection policy, and all approved establishments will feature a green pass sign in the window. Tap water is safe to drink. Many pharmacies are open around the clock or until midnight. **Shoppers Drug Mart** (ⓐ 465 Yonge St ① 416-408-4000 Ⓦ www.shoppersdrugmart.ca Ⓝ Subway: College; streetcar: 506 Carlton) is open 24 hours a day, with other late-night locations at King and Spadina (ⓐ 388 King St W ① 416-597-6550 🕓 08.00–00.00 Ⓝ Subway: St. Andrew; streetcar: 504 King, 510 Spadina) and right by the Harbourfront (ⓐ 390 Queen's Quay W ① 416-260-2766 🕓 08.00–00.00 Ⓝ Subway: Union; streetcar: 504 King). The authorities occasionally issue smog warnings in summer, meaning that you should stay out of the sun if possible and avoid strenuous exercise outdoors.

Canada's healthcare system is good and free to citizens, but costs can be steep for foreign patients and payment is required upfront. Ensure you take out adequate medical insurance in your home country before arriving in Canada.

In comparison to many North American and smaller Canadian cities, Toronto is quite safe. Police can often be seen riding bikes, horses and cars throughout the city. The streets tend to empty out on weeknights by 23.00 and on weekends by 01.00; after this time, it's best to take public transport or a taxi rather than walking back to your accommodation. If you do walk at night, don't listen to an iPod, as these are targeted by muggers. Bike theft is rampant in Toronto, so make sure to lock all rented bikes to the inside bar of the street bike posts.

OPENING HOURS

The first businesses to open in Toronto are the cafés, which start serving at 07.00 on weekdays and a little later at weekends. Shops generally open around 10.00 throughout the week and close at 20.00 or 21.00. Smaller shops may not open until midday and often have sporadic hours. Banks open around 09.00 and often stay open as late as 19.00 or 20.00.

Restaurants usually either cater to the lunch crowd (opening at 07.00 and closing at 15.00) or to the dinner crowd (opening at 18.00 and closing at 23.00), although some remain open all day. Most bars open at 16.00 for after-work drinks and close at around 02.00. Nightclubs are the last to close, usually between 02.00 and 04.00. For public transport hours, see page 56.

TOILETS

The best places to scout out toilets are shopping centres such as the Eaton Centre (see page 70) and public libraries. These facilities are clean, well-lit and well-stocked. Restaurants and bars all have facilities, but if you're not planning to have a drink or something to eat there, it's polite to ask before using them.

CHILDREN

In the last three to four years, Toronto has filled up with young families eager to raise their kids in this vibrant city. These new families have even carved out neighbourhoods for themselves. Head to the Roncesvalles, Leslieville and Parkdale neighbourhoods (see pages 76 & 92) for kid-friendly cafés, restaurants and shopping. Using public transport is generally not a problem with children, although be aware that not all subway stations in the Downtown core are stroller friendly.

There are plenty of activities to keep kids amused, even in fairly unlikely places such as museums. In the Royal Ontario Museum (see page 68), a purpose-built Discovery Area offers kids under the age of five the chance to dig amongst the sand for dinosaur bones, dress in costumes, or play around with the puzzles and games provided. In the same museum is the Family Gallery for slightly older kids, who will appreciate the biodiversity displays. Not as crowded as the ROM and possibly more interesting for children with a scientific bent is the **Ontario Science Centre** (ⓐ 770 Don Mills Rd ⓣ 416-696-1000 ⓦ www.ontariosciencecentre.ca ⓛ 10.00–18.00 Fri–Wed, 10.00–20.00 Thur. Admission charge), which has a great selection of exhibits for kids aged ten or over who can appreciate playing music with a fountain or racing with wheelchairs. And if you just need a bit of family chilling time, head to Riverdale Farm (see page 44).

A general rule is that the pricier a restaurant is, the less likely it is that babies or young children are welcome. No young children are allowed in bars. Restaurants that are particularly child-friendly include **Dakota Tavern** (£ ⓐ 249 Ossington Ave ❶ 416-850-4579 ⓦ www.thedakotatavern.com ❶ 18.00–02.00 Mon–Fri, 15.00–02.00 Sat, 11.00–15.00, 18.00–02.00 Sun), known for its Bluegrass Brunch on Sunday mornings during which a lively band plays, and **Mitzi's Sister** (£ ⓐ 1554 Queen St W ❶ 416-532-2570 ⓦ www.mitzissister.com ❶ 16.00–02.00 Mon–Fri, 10.00–02.00 Sat & Sun) in Parkdale, which has a great breakfast menu.

COMMUNICATIONS
Internet
It's easy to get online if you have a laptop, since many cafés offer free wireless internet access with purchase. Many free wireless spots are run by the not-for-profit group **Wireless Toronto** (ⓦ http://wirelesstoronto.ca), which has a list of hotspots on their website including **Toronto Reference Library** (ⓐ 789 Yonge St ❶ 416-395-5577 ⓦ www.torontopubliclibrary.ca ❶ 09.30–20.30 Mon–Thur, 09.30–17.30 Fri, 09.00–17.00 Sat; also open 13.30–17.30 Sun, Sept–June ⓝ Subway: Bloor, Bay), St Lawrence Market and Yonge-Dundas Square. Log in under the network name 'wirelesstoronto'. There is 24-hour internet access at **Net Effect Café** (ⓐ 9 Isabella St ❶ 416-964-0749) and **Web Fusion** (ⓐ 545 Sherbourne St ❶ 416-925-5104).

TELEPHONING CANADA

To call Canada from abroad, dial your country's international calling code (00 from the UK) followed by 1 and the ten-digit number you wish to call.

TELEPHONING ABROAD

To make an international call from Canada, dial 011 followed by the country code, area code (usually dropping the first 'o' if there is one) and the local number you wish to call. Country codes include: UK 44, Republic of Ireland 353, USA 1, Australia 61, New Zealand 64 and South Africa 27.

Phone

Phone numbers in Toronto have ten digits, all of which must be dialled even when making a local call. The first three digits are the area code, which in Toronto is usually 416 for landlines and 647 for mobile phones and some business numbers. When making a long-distance phone call outside of the Toronto metropolitan area, dial 1 before the ten-digit number. 1-800 and 1-888 numbers are usually toll-free.

Post

Post offices and red post boxes are identified by their red and blue Canada Post logo. There are sometimes post office branches inside drug and convenience stores.

ELECTRICITY

Voltage is 110–120 volts, 60 hertz and electrical plugs are the

two-pin type used in the US. Visitors from the US will not need any special equipment, but those from the UK, Europe, South Africa and Australia will require an adaptor.

TRAVELLERS WITH DISABILITIES

Most public transport in Toronto is now wheelchair accessible: check the official **Toronto Transit Commission** website (ⓦ www3.ttc.ca) and click 'Accessibility' for comprehensive, up-to-date information. All GO Transit trains (see page 129) have one carriage with a wheelchair ramp and over half of the GO Transit stations are accessible. Many larger hotels have at least one accessible room, but it's wise to be absolutely clear about your requirements when booking. Those who are more adventurous can go camping in **Ontario Parks** (ⓦ www.ontarioparks.com), which offers reduced rates for travellers with disabilities. The Travellers' Aid Society (see opposite) can offer guidance and advice to travellers with disabilities as well as assist them on arrival. There are Travellers' Aid booths at all three Terminals of Toronto Pearson International Airport as well as in Union Station.

TOURIST INFORMATION

Toronto's official tourist board is **Tourism Toronto** (ⓐ 207 Queens Quay West, Downtown ⓣ 416-203-2500 ⓦ www.seetorontonow.com ⓛ 08.30–18.00 Mon–Fri). Their comprehensive website contains much of the information you need to plan your trip, from accommodation listings to a calendar of forthcoming events. The City of Toronto also operate a **Travel Information Centre** (ⓐ 20 Dundas St W ⓣ 416-392-9300) and offer a host of useful information for both residents and visitors on their website ⓦ www.toronto.ca.

The not-for-profit **Travellers' Aid Society** (ⓣ 416-366-7788 ⓦ www.travellersaid.ca) has booths at Toronto Pearson International Airport as well as the railway station and can help Toronto visitors with anything from last-minute reservations to emergency health advice.

Good blogs to read are *Spacing Magazine* (ⓦ http://spacing.ca/wire), which covers public space issues, as well as *Torontoist* (ⓦ http://torontoist.com) and *BlogTO* (ⓦ www.blogto.com) that focus on alternative news and events. For events listings, see page 28.

BACKGROUND READING

In the Skin of a Lion by Michael Ondaatje. Set in Toronto in the early 20th century, Ondaatje's novel offers a part-fictional, part-historical view of the city.

Toronto Life magazine covers the food scene with a watchful eye and also runs longer, general interest pieces on ongoing city issues.

uTOpia: Towards a New Toronto edited by Alana Wilcox and Jason McBride. A compilation of essays about the city's identity by local writers, thinkers and artists.

Emergencies

In any emergency, dial  911. This free number connects to an operator who will direct your call to the appropriate service.

MEDICAL SERVICES

See ⓦ www.hco-on.ca for a list of walk-in clinics in Toronto. Note that you will have to pay for treatment upfront, so ensure you have adequate medical insurance. Another option is to call **Telehealth Ontario** (ⓣ 1-866-797-0000 ⓦ www.health.gov.on.ca), a free, 24-hour health advisory phone line.

Hospitals

St Michael's Hospital ⓐ 30 Bond St ⓣ 416-360-4000 ⓦ www.stmichaelshospital.com Ⓝ Subway: Dundas, Queen; streetcar: 501 Queen, 505 Dundas

Toronto General Hospital ⓐ 200 Elizabeth St ⓣ 416-340-3946 ⓦ www.uhn.ca Ⓝ Subway: Queen's Park, St. Patrick, Dundas; streetcar: 505 Dundas, 506 Carlton

Emergency dentist

Dental Emergency Service ⓐ 1650 Yonge St ⓣ 416-485-7121 ⓛ 08.00–00.00 Ⓝ Subway: St. Clair West; streetcar: 512 St Clair

POLICE

If it is not an emergency, you can contact the police on ⓣ 416-808-2222 or see ⓦ www.torontopolice.on.ca. There are various police stations around town. In Downtown, go to the

Area Field location (📍 40 College St ☎ 416-808-2222 🚇 Subway: College, streetcar: 506 Carlton). For the West End, head to the **Parkdale Community Policing Centre** (📍 1303 Queen St W ☎ 416-808-1410 🚇 Streetcar: 501 Queen; bus: 29 Dufferin, 47 Lansdowne). In the East End, there's **51 Division** (☎ 51 Parliament St ☎ 416-808-5108 🚇 Subway: King; streetcar: 504 King).

EMBASSIES & CONSULATES

Australian Consulate-General 📍 175 Bloor St E ☎ 416-323-1155 🌐 www.dfat.gov.au 🕐 09.00–13.00, 14.00–16.30 Mon–Fri 🚇 Subway: Bloor, Sherbourne

British Consulate-General 📍 777 Bay St ☎ 416-593-1290 🌐 http://ukincanada.fco.gov.uk 🚇 Subway: College, Queen's Park; streetcar: 506 Carlton

New Zealand Honourary Consul 📍 965 Bay St ☎ 416-947-9696 🌐 www.nzembassy.com 🕐 09.00–10.30, 13.30–16.30 Mon–Fri 🚇 Subway: Wellesley, Bloor; bus: 94 Wellesley

South African Consulate-General 📍 110 Sheppard Ave E ☎ 416-944-8825 🌐 www.sacgtoronto.com 🚇 Subway: Sheppard-Yonge, bus: 85 Sheppard Avenue East

United States Embassy 📍 360 University Ave ☎ Office hours: 416-595-1700; emergencies: 416-595-6506 🌐 www.consular. canada.usembassy.gov 🕐 08.15–15.00 Mon–Fri 🚇 Subway: Osgoode, Queen, St. Patrick; streetcar: 501 Queen

A

accommodation 34–9
  Niagara region 117
  Stratford 126
air travel 48–9, 128
Algonquin
  Provincial Park 32–3
Amish Mennonite
  community 121
Art Gallery of Ontario
  (AGO) 20, 66–7
arts see culture

B

background reading 137
bars & clubs see nightlife
Bata Shoe Museum 67
breweries 46–7, 64
bus travel 52, 56, 110–11, 129

C

cafés
  Downtown 72–3
  East End 98–101
  Niagara region 116–17
  Stratford 125–6
  West End 86–7
car hire 56
Casa Loma 58–62
Centreville
  Amusement Park 66
children 133–4
Chinatown 62
cinemas 10, 28–9
City Hall, Stratford 120–1

climate 8
CN Tower 62
crime 131–2
culture 18–20
customs & duty 130
cycling 53, 110

D

dance 67
disabled travellers 136
Distillery District 64
Don Jail 92–3
Downtown 58–75
driving 52, 56, 111, 129–30
Dufferin Grove Park 76–80

E

East Chinatown 93
East End 92–104
Eaton Centre 70
electricity 135–6
embassies &
  consulates 139
emergencies 138–9
entertainment 28–9
  see also nightlife
events & festivals 8–11,
  116, 118–20, 123

F

Factory 163 124
Fleck Dance Theatre 67
food & drink 24–7, 99
Fort George 113
Fort York 64

G

Gallery Stratford 124
Gardiner Museum of
  Ceramic Art 67–8
Gerrard India Bazaar 96
Greektown 96

H

health 131, 138–9
High Park 80
history 14–15
Hockey Hall of Fame 64–5
hotels see
  accommodation

I

internet 134

J

Journey Behind
  the Falls 112

K

Katherine Mulherin
  Contemporary
  Art Projects 81–2
Kensington Market 71

L

Laura Secord
  Homestead 114
lifestyle 16–17
listings 28

M

Maid of the Mist 112
markets 44, 62, 71, 123–4
money 130–1

money-saving cards 22
Museum of
   Contemporary
   Canadian Art
   (MOCCA) 82
music 9, 18–20, 28, 68,
   104, 118–20
Music Gallery 68

N
Nathan Phillips Square 65
Niagara Falls 111–13
Niagara Historical Society
   Museum 114–16
Niagara-on-the-Lake 113–17
Niagara region 106–17
Niagara's Fury 112–13
nightlife 28–9
   Downtown 73–4
   East End 102–4
   West End 89–91

O
Ontario Crafts Council 82
Ontario Science Centre 133
opening hours 132

P
passports & visas 130
phones 135
picnics 44, 71, 80, 118
police 132, 139
post 135
Power Plant
   Contemporary
   Art Gallery 68

public holidays 11
public transport 48–53,
   56, 110–11, 120, 128–9

Q
Queen Street West 12–13,
   18, 23, 76

R
rail travel 52, 110, 128–9
restaurants
   Downtown 73
   East End 102–3
   Niagara region 116–17
   Stratford 125–6
   West End 89
Riverdale Farm 44
Rogers Centre 65
Royal Conservatory
   of Music 20
Royal Ontario Museum
   (ROM) 20, 68

S
safety 53, 131–2
seasons 8
Shakespeare Festival 123
Shaw Festival 116
shopping 22–3
   Downtown 70–1
   East End 96–8
   Stratford 124–5
   West End 83–4
sport & activities 30–1
St Lawrence Market 71

Stephen Bulger
   Gallery 82–3
Stratford 118–26
street food 27
symbols &
   abbreviations 4

T
taxis 48, 56
theatre 10, 18, 29, 67,
   116, 123
time difference 48
tipping 27
toilets 132
Toronto Dominion
   Centre 65–6
Toronto Islands 66
tourist information 136–7
tours 32, 112–13
Trinity Bellwoods
   Park 80–1

W
weather 8, 46–7
West End 76–91
White Water Walk 113
wine tours 115–16

ACKNOWLEDGEMENTS & FEEDBACK

Editorial/project management: Lisa Plumridge
Copy editor: Monica Guy
Layout/DTP: Alison Rayner

The publishers would like to thank the following for supplying their copyright photographs for this book: BigStockPhoto.com (Gary Blakeley, pages 57 & 69; Christopher Chang, page 49; Lucy Cherniak, page 129; Elena Elisseeva, pages 5, 33, 43, 45 & 105; David Francisco, page 47; Alexandar Iotzov, page 122; Mike Lee, page 9; Chiya Li, pages 40–1; Horst Petzold, page 7; Massimiliano Pieraccini, page 15; Samuel Shpiro, pages 13 & 127; Artem Svystun, page 59; Lorraine Swanson, page 107; Graça Victoria, page 63); Laurence Cymet, page 97; John F, page 119; Chris Fore, page 21; Richard Hsu, page 23; imaging brain, page 93; Imnop88a, page 26; Andrew Louis, page 29; Matt MacGillivray, pages 17, 25 & 87; Craige Moore, page 75; Muhammad, page 85; Ian Muttoo, page 19; Alison

Send your thoughts to
books@thomascook.com

- Found a great bar, club, shop or must-see sight that we don't feature?
- Like to tip us off about any information that needs a little updating?
- Want to tell us what you love about this handy little guidebook and more importantly how we can make it even handier?

Then here's your chance to tell all! Send us ideas, discoveries and recommendations today and then look out for your valuable input in the next edition of this title.

Email the above address (stating the title) or write to:
pocket guides Series Editor, Thomas Cook Publishing, PO Box 227, Coningsby Road, Peterborough PE3 8SB, UK.

WHAT'S IN YOUR GUIDEBOOK?

Independent authors Impartial up-to-date information from our travel experts who meticulously source local knowledge.

Experience Thomas Cook's 165 years in the travel industry and guidebook publishing enriches every word with expertise you can trust.

Travel know-how Thomas Cook has thousands of staff working around the globe, all living and breathing travel.

Editors Travel-publishing professionals, pulling everything together to craft a perfect blend of words, pictures, maps and design.

You, the traveller We deliver a practical, no-nonsense approach to information, geared to how you really use it.

Rayner, page 114; Diego Silvestre, page 77; sookie, page 36; Angie Torres, pages 35 & 101; Gary J. Wood, page 81; Ed Yourdon, page 88.

ABOUT THE AUTHOR

Laura Trethewey is a native Torontonian, born and raised. After travelling extensively through Europe and North America, she has settled in her hometown where she works as a freelance writer. She has worked for city publications such as *Toronto Life* magazine, and written for *The Globe and Mail* and *Torontoist*.